Praise for
Jesus, Buddha, Krishna & Lao Tzu

"A priceless treasury of interfaith understanding."

—Brother David Steindl-Rast, O.S.B.

"I was much taken by the idea of this book when I first learned it was in the making, but the execution of it—the reality of it—is just wonderful. Its publication is a truly timely event, bound to nourish those who are soul-weary of combativeness in the name of religion."

—Carol Lee Flinders, PhD, author of
Enduring Lives: Portrait of Women and Faith in Action

"Richard Hooper sends a powerful message that will be welcomed by all who seek the truth within, and within their own tradition."

—Jeff Cox, Snow Lion Publications

"Richard Hooper shatters any preconceived notions that there is only 'one way' to enlightenment. Instead, he blazes a path of collective understanding beyond dogma toward finding the divinity within ourselves."

—Judy Martin, Emmy Award-winning radio journalist
and founder of WorkLifeMonitor.com

JESUS, BUDDHA, KRISHNA & LAO TZU

THE PARALLEL SAYINGS

JESUS, BUDDHA, KRISHNA & LAO TZU

THE PARALLEL SAYINGS

Edited and with an introduction by

Richard J. Hooper

BRISTOL PARK BOOKS / NEW YORK

Originally published as *Jesus, Buddha, Krishna, Lao Tzu* in 2007
By Sanctuary Publications

Credits; p. 116 from the Online Collection of the Brooklyn Museum;
Photo: 37.122_IMLS_SL2.jpg; p. 127, Buddha, Dhyana Mudra,
Michael Hoefner, http://www.zwo5.de
p. 159, Statutes in Meenakshi Amman Temple Tower

First Bristol Park Books edition published in 2013

Bristol Park Books
252 W. 38th Street
NYC, NY 10018

Bristol Park Books is a registered trademark of Bristol Park
Books, Inc.

Published by arrangement with Hampton Roads Publishing Company

ISBN: 978-0-88486-549-0

Cover Design: Barb Fisher
Interior Design by Kathryn Sky-Peck

Printed in the United States of America

Dedicated to the memory of
Eknath Easwaran,
a true wise man from the East

Contents

You must make the effort yourself. The masters only point the way.

—The Buddha

Introduction

If the doors of perception were cleansed,
everything would appear to man as it is, infinite.
For man has closed himself up, till he sees all things
through narrow chinks of his cavern.

—William Blake, *The Marriage of Heaven and Hell*

THE MYSTICAL IMPERATIVE

The story goes that, after his enlightenment, Siddhartha Gautama—the historical Buddha—was walking down the road when he met a fellow traveler. The other man perceived a great radiance emanating from Siddhartha, so instead of asking, "Who are you," he asked, "Are you a god or a divine being?" "No," answered the Buddha. "Are you a shaman or a sorcerer?" "No," answered the Buddha. "Are you a man?" Again the Buddha answered, "No." "Well, then," the man said, "what are you?" The Buddha answered, "I am awake." And, indeed, this is what "Buddha" means: one who is awakened.

According to the Gospels of the *New Testament*, much the same thing happened in the case of Jesus. Siddhartha was tempted by Mara, the Evil One, and when he achieved victory over all temptations, he instantly "woke up." The story of Jesus' temptation in the wilderness is almost a carbon copy of the Buddha legend. Jesus, like the Buddha, was victorious over all the temptations presented to him by "Satan," and in the moment of his victory, he was utterly changed. As he walked by the seashore, fishermen saw his radiance, dropped their nets and followed him. As he walked through pastures and fields, farmers let go of their plows and followed him.

As with the Buddha, everyone who met Jesus knew he was no ordinary man. What made these two men special? For one thing, they both had profound wisdom. But their wisdom was unlike others because it came, not from intellectual reasoning, but from direct awareness of the Absolute. Jesus and the Buddha were mystics. Their teachings carried the weight of authority because they came from the source of being itself. Their personal wisdom was not the result of religious belief or faith, but came from a place of *gnosis*—knowledge. Both Jesus and the Buddha were plugged into "the Source."

A century ago William James in *The Varieties of Religious Experience* observed, " . . . mystical states seem to those who experience them to be states of knowledge. They are states of sight into depths of truth unplumbed by the discursive intellect . . . and as a rule they carry with them a curious sense of authority for aftertime."[1]

The Gospel stories about Jesus, for instance, claim that those who heard him were amazed that he spoke with "authority," not like the priests or the other teachers of his day. Had Jesus not had charisma, wisdom, and *knowledge*, it is highly doubtful anyone would have remembered his words.

People who met the Buddha knew immediately that he had had some profound experience, and that the experience had altogether altered him. Like Jesus, when the Buddha spoke, people listened because they recognized his words as coming from somewhere other than the intellectual mind. They seemed to come from the Source of understanding itself.

I first read the words of Krishna in the *Bhagavad Gita* some forty years ago. At the time, I was still very much a committed and believing Christian—heading to seminary after college. Yet I found myself fascinated with Krishna's words in the same way that I was with Jesus'. Those words didn't seem to agree with Christian dogmas but, for

---

1 William James, *The Varieties of Religious Experience*, Collier Macmillan, New York, 1961, p. 300.

me, they had the ring of truth. When I later read the teachings attributed to Lao Tzu in the *Tao Te Ching*, I had the very same reaction. The interior heart of understanding can recognize "truth" in an instant.

Even though these teachers represent four different world religions, I believe their teachings have a great deal in common. Could it be that their teachings represent four slightly different paths to the same destination? Each of these masters claimed that their teachings came from personal experience of ultimate reality, so we might expect their teachings to be similar. Certainly their teachings carry the weight of authority—in our day, as well as theirs.

If the words of certain teachers move us, and if we were to examine our thoughts while reading them, what often strikes us most is not that these teachers are telling us something new, but that they are reminding us of something we already knew but, perhaps, had forgotten. It is as if we had always known these truths at some deep level, so we respond with, "Aha!" "Yes, of course. I knew that all along." These teachers reveal the truth that has always been within us.

But the teachings that come from those in touch with the Absolute still have limitations. Mystical insight has the nature of ineffability. Direct awareness of Ultimate Reality—and for our purposes we will assume that's what it is—can never be adequately communicated in words. James says of the mystical experience, "The subject of it immediately says that it defies expression, that no adequate report of its contents can be given in words."[2] The most any mystic can do is to convey approximations of his or her experience. Teaching, therefore, often takes the form of negation: "Not this, not that."

---

2 Ibid, pp. 299-300.

Certainly history has had many mystics who didn't try to communicate their understanding to others. Others have tried and failed. In the case of Jesus, for instance, the canonical Gospels make it clear that even his closest disciples didn't "get it" much of the time. Teachers may do their very best to convey mystical insight using parables, dialectic, symbolism, and other forms of wisdom teaching, but in the end, the words will always fall short of the reality. So the words of even the greatest teachers are, at best, no more than road signs on the path to understanding. They are, more often than not, cautionary: Yield; Watch for falling rocks; Slow down, you're going the wrong way.

Every true teacher knows that all those who follow them must seek enlightenment through their own personal efforts, in their own individual way. The teacher can give advice, prescribe methodology, and steer the student away from unproductive paths, but in the end—everyone is on their own.

This is the limitation of organized religion as well. Once the teacher is gone, all bets are off. Religious devotees have a tendency to codify their teachers' wisdom, but in doing so they turn living truth into a pale transparency of itself. The moment anyone's teachings become packaged for mass consumption, the essence of those teachings are lost to one degree or another.

Official canons, while important, can often short circuit the effectiveness of a spiritual path, and even create deception. Certainly this happens when the teacher is elevated to divine status and worshiped as Truth itself. This is why Buddhists say such things as, "Do not seek the Buddha, seek what the Buddha sought," or, "If you meet the Buddha on the road, kill him."

Jesus told his followers that the answer was within *themselves*: "If those who lead you say the Kingdom of heaven is in the sky, then the birds of the sky will get there before you do. If they say it is in the sea, then the fish will beat you there. Rather, the kingdom is within you…"[3] Every teaching, every word—no matter how profound—is only a guidepost along the way. Every seeker is a pilgrim, and every pilgrim travels alone.

---

3 The Gospel of Thomas, 3a.

THE VALUE AND LIMITATION OF WORDS

Nevertheless, I think teachings are important. They guide us and inspire us, and they represent humanity's common effort to seek knowledge. Ultimately—and I think most teachers would agree—the teachings are more important than the teacher. That's important to mention here because *the words attributed to Jesus, Krishna, the Buddha, and Lao Tzu did not necessarily originate with those men.*

Of the four, only Jesus and the Buddha are considered to be historical figures. As an avatar, Krishna (Hinduism considers the Buddha and Jesus to be avatars as well) is the mythical incarnation of Ishvara—a personal deity who, in turn, is an emanation of Brahman, the ultimate Godhead. And while there is a "history" of the Chinese sage, Lao Tzu—a name that simply means "old master"—most scholars do not take it seriously, and believe the *Tao Te Ching* was written anonymously.

In fact, all the texts that we will consider here were written anonymously. The Gospels, for instance, have no authors' names attached. These works were simply attributed to Matthew, Mark, Luke, and John by Christians at a later date as a matter of Christian tradition. Moreover, Jesus spoke in Aramaic, and all of the books of the *New Testament* were written in Greek.

In the case of Siddhartha Gautama, the historical Buddha, none of his actual words remain. Siddhartha spoke Ardhamagadhi, and none of his sayings are preserved in that form. All that remains are translations of the earliest Buddhist canons; and since Buddhism, like Christianity, began as an oral tradition, the Buddha's actual words are lost to us.

We know somewhat more about the words of the historical Jesus, but not nearly as much as most Christians think. The four canonical Gospels were written by Greek speaking Christians, and the dates of their composition date between 70 C.E. and 120 C.E. None of the Gospel authors were eye-witnesses to the life and teachings of Jesus. It is also unlikely that they even knew any of the original eye-witnesses since they wrote their Gospels long after Jesus' disciples would still be alive, and they wrote them far from the land of Palestine.

Most of what appears in the canonical Gospels is Christian mythology, not Jewish history. Ancient mythologists (and that includes Hindus, Buddhists, and Taoists) thought nothing of putting their own words into their teachers' mouths, and in the case of Jesus, they made him a Christian retrospectively. The historical Jesus did not believe himself to be the Messiah, or son of God, as is borne out by the earliest "source" gospels.[4]

Certain groups of *New Testament* scholars, such as the Jesus Seminar, suggest that as few as 18 percent of all the words attributed to Jesus in the canonical Gospels actually came from him, and even these are probably not in their original form. In the case of the apocryphal and Gnostic Gospels, the problem is even more pronounced.

In spite of all this, those who invented the words attributed to Jesus, Krishna, the Buddha, and Lao Tzu believed that they were writing *in the spirit* of these great teachers—which is to say, the anonymous authors of each text believed that their teacher would have said these words had he been given the opportunity.

The ancient mythologists were anything but literalists, believing that the words they put in their teacher's mouth were *true*, even if they weren't *historical*. And perhaps this is a good guide for the reader as well. If the words in this book have the ring of truth, then it probably doesn't matter *who* originally said or wrote them.

WISE MEN FROM THE EAST

I have wanted to present a comparison of Jesus' teachings with those of the Eastern masters for a long time—in fact, ever since I was introduced to Eastern philosophy in college. As a young man headed to seminary after graduation, I wanted to know what the teachers of other religions had to say, so I took a major in Eastern and Western philosophy. Though I didn't know it at the time, I had set myself on a path that would eventually lead right out the back door of the Church. Yet my disagreements with "orthodox" Christianity began as a child.

---

4 Two source Gospels, the Gospel known as "Q", aka the *Synoptic Sayings Source*, and parts of *The Gospel of Thomas* were written as early as 50 C.E., and show no evidence of "Christian" teachings.

I recall one night—I was about twelve years of age—when the pastor of our church was talking to our youth group. He was telling us that anyone who did not believe in Jesus would not go to heaven, intimating that they would go to that *other* place instead. This statement shocked me.

I raised my hand and asked the pastor, "Do you mean to say that even someone living in a faraway place like India, who has never even heard of Jesus, will go to hell because they don't believe in him?" To my utter amazement, the pastor answered in the affirmative.

I couldn't believe my ears. I knew I was just a kid, but I thought that this was the dumbest thing I ever heard. I respected the pastor and believed that he must be in contact with truth at some level, but in this case I knew in my heart that he was wrong. Since I believed in Jesus, I also believed in his Father—who Jesus described as a God of love and compassion. So I chose to believe Jesus rather than my pastor because I could not accept that a loving God would be so unfair as to actually send people to hell for no good reason.

Many people who are interested in Eastern philosophy have probably had similar experiences while growing up in the Christian Church. Their own personal disconnects may have caused them to start questioning the dogmas of the Church, and whether or not Christianity really reflects the teachings of Jesus. Many people may sense that the religion *about* Jesus is quite different than the religion *of* Jesus.

Such criticisms of Christianity are hardly new. Ever since the Enlightenment, thoughtful Christians have been asking whether the teachings of the Church have any real relationship to the man upon whom the Church was supposedly founded. In 1884, Leo Tolstoy published a book titled *My Religion*, and his words probably reflect the views of many former Christians:

> From my childhood, from the time I first began to read the *New Testament*, I was touched most of all by that portion of the doctrine of Jesus which inculcates love, humility, self-denial, and the duty of returning good for evil. This, to me, has always been the substance of Christianity; my heart recognized its truth in spite of skepticism and despair, and for this reason I submitted to a

religion professed by a multitude of toilers, who find in it the solution of life—the religion taught by the Orthodox Church. But in making my submission to the Church, I soon saw that I should not find in its creed the confirmation of the essence of Christianity; what was to me essential seemed to be in the dogma of the Church merely an accessory. What was to me the most important teachings of Jesus was not so regarded by the Church... What I found most repulsive in the doctrine of the Church was the strangeness of its dogmas and the approval, nay, the support, which it gave to persecutions, to the death penalty, to wars stirred up by the intolerance common to all sects; but my faith was chiefly shattered by the indifference of the Church to what seemed to me essential in the teachings of Jesus...[5]

Tolstoy's disconnect with the Church began to form in his mind even as a child. This is not surprising since children can be quite sensitive to hypocrisy. Tolstoy speaks for many of us who have left the Church, but have *not* turned away from Jesus. While the Church may have been found wanting, Jesus still speaks to the ages.

As the age of unbelief dawned in the West, a wave of exotic religious ideas from Eastern religions began to wash up on the shores of Europe and America, giving Christians and former Christians the chance to compare the teachings of Jesus with the teachings of Eastern religions—especially Hinduism.

Theosophy became a major Western philosophical movement during the nineteenth century, and many, if not most, of its ideas were drawn from Hinduism. Karma, reincarnation, and the study of the chakras of the human body all came to the West via India during the nineteenth century. The translation of Hinduism's most sacred text, the *Bhagavad Gita* (*The Lord's Song*) into English during that century even influenced such great authors as Emerson and Thoreau.

A second wave of Hinduism washed ashore when Swami Vivekananda established the Vedanta Society in New York in 1894, and Paramahansa Yogananda founded a yoga institute in Los Angeles in 1925 (which would later become the Self-Realization Fellow-

---

5 Count Leo N. Tolstoy, *My Religion*, London, Walter Scott Publishing, pp. 2-3.

INTRODUCTION

ship.) The teachings of Shankara and Ramakrishna, the Yoga Aphorisms of Patanjali, all became established—albeit in a small way—in Western culture.

The path was thus prepared for yet another invasion of holy men from the East beginning in the 1960s. The Maharishi Mahesh Yogi popularized the practice of meditation, and counted as his early disciples such entertainment luminaries as the Beatles, Clint Eastwood, Mia Farrow, and Merv Griffin. Swami Satchidananda gave the invocation at the Woodstock Festival in 1969. Swami Muktananda, Krishnamurti, Sri Chinmoy, Satya Sai Baba, Bhagwan Shree Rajneesh, Eknath Easwaran, and a host of other Hindu teachers all had tremendous influence on the Counter Culture movement of the 1960s and '70s.

Arriving during this same time period, in much smaller numbers, were the missionaries of Buddhism. The great Rinzai master Soyen Shaku introduced Zen Buddhism to America in 1893. The Zen authors D.T. Suzuki and Shunryu Suzuki Roshi provided the foundation of Zen thought for thousands of readers during the twentieth century. The Tibetan Buddhist lama, Chogyam Trungpa Rinpoche, along with many other lamas, popularized Tibetan Buddhism in the United States during the second half of the twentieth century. It would be hard to find anyone in the West today who has not at least heard of the Dalai Lama—the world's foremost ambassador of good will. The West has also produced its own "Eastern" teachers: Alan Watts, Ram Dass, Richard Baker Roshi, and scores of others.

Taoism—a Chinese philosophy that dates back thousands of years—did not send its missionaries to the West, but its influence has been felt nonetheless. Most Westerners are primarily familiar with ancient Taoism through two books: the *Tao Te Ching* and the *Tao of Chuang Tzu*. But Taoist principles are also found in the oracle, the *I Ching* (*The Book of Change*), in the practice of Tai Chi Chuan, in acupuncture, and in Chinese medicine. The symbol of the Tao—the yin/yang—can be seen virtually everywhere in the United States, and with "the Force" of *Star Wars* fame, movie producer George Lucas popularized the science fiction version of Tao.

If the old religions of Western culture have failed to provide meaning for many people today, can Eastern religions do any better? Only time will tell. To date it seems that their primary influence has not been in the form of establishing outposts, but in influencing non-traditional movements, which have repackaged Eastern philosophy to fit a different time, a different land, and a different culture. Certainly the New Age movement is chief among such repackaging centers, and has all but become a religion in itself.

As the New Age movement has evolved (some would say, devolved) since the 1970s, much of it has often wandered off into realms of new mythologies, super-stition, and the occult. In spite of this rather discouraging trend, many "new age" principles are firmly founded on the basic insights of Eastern philosophy. This new religious culture in the West has made its own contributions as well. While classic religious texts produced by the religions of the East are not read by most people today, most Hindu, Buddhist, and Taoist teachings in the West in our present age come from Western authors who, while being directly influenced by Eastern religions, have reformulated ancient truths for modern times and Western sensibilities. Even those books written by Buddhist monks, Tibetan lamas, and Indian gurus are written to appeal to the modern—Western—reader. It would seem that in every age, that which is old must be made new again.

Of course, few spiritual insights are ever *really* new. The anonymous author who called himself "the Preacher" addressed this in the Biblical book of *Ecclesiastes*:

> What has been is what will be, and what has been done is what will be done; and there is nothing new under the sun. Is there a thing of which it is said, "See, this is new?" It has been already, in the ages before us. There is no remembrance of former things, nor is there any remembrance of later things yet to happen among those who come after.[6]

The Preacher was a pessimist perhaps, but he had a point. Science has the poten-tial to change our worldview, but there really isn't anything new under the sun when it concerns religion, philosophy, and metaphysics. Every insight has been revealed before by someone, somewhere. And while it is often helpful to reformulate age-old teachings, it is also useful to reread the classic texts of religion, which are themselves the product

6 *Ecclesiastes* 1:8–11.

of numerous sages over great spans of time. For some readers, the wisdom of the ages makes the most sense coming in the words of the original masters, hence this book.

EAST MEETS WEST

When comparing the insights of different teachers we find either similarities or dissimilarities, or a combination of both. Dissimilarity is to be expected and is easily explainable: different teacher, different religion and culture, and different periods of time.

Similarities, on the other hand, often do call out for an explanation. How is it that two teachers who lived during different eras, in countries widely separated, and whose religions and cultures were quite different, make almost identical statements about spirituality and the meaning of life? Immediately the historian and the theologian will suspect a causal link. One philosophy or religion must have influenced another. More often than not, these suspicions turn out to be correct.

There is no question that Hinduism was the foundation for Buddhism. Siddhartha Gautama was born in India, and Buddhism in the beginning was considered just another Hindu sect. For the first two hundred and fifty years of its existence, Buddhism's influence was strictly limited to the borders of India. By the time of its first missionary success in Ceylon, around 240 C.E., Buddhism had already broken down into a number of sects. Each sect produced new literature, and the words of those texts were attributed to the historical Buddha.

Buddhism and Hinduism certainly had some influence on Greek philosophy, and Greek philosophy, in turn, influenced first century Judaism, early orthodox Christianity and Gnosticism. But Buddhism and Hinduism may have had a more direct influence on Gnostic Christianity.

More than thirty years ago, Elaine Pagels in her seminal study, *The Gnostic Gospels*, asked whether Gnostic Christianity might have been directly influenced by these two Eastern religions:

> Could Hindu or Buddhist traditions have influenced Gnosticism? The British scholar of Buddhism, Edward Conze, suggests that it had. He points out that

"Buddhists were in contact with the Thomas Christians (that is, Christians who knew and used such writings as the *Gospel of Thomas*) in South India." Trade routes between the Greco-Roman world and the Far East were opening up at the time when Gnosticism flourished (C.E. 80–200); for generations, Buddhist missionaries had been proselytizing in Alexandria. We note, too, that Hippolytus, who was a Greek speaking Christian in Rome (around 225 C.E.), knows of Indian Brahmins—and includes their tradition among the sources of heresy. . . . Could the title of the *Gospel of Thomas*—named for the disciple who, tradition tells us, went to India—suggest the influence of Indian tradition? These hints indicate the possibility, yet our evidence is not conclusive. Since parallel traditions may emerge in different cultures at different times, such ideas could have developed in both places independently.[7]

Only time will tell if scholars can tease out more evidence of direct influence. But while there are shreds of evidence suggesting a possible connection between Hinduism and Buddhism and Christian Gnosticism, there is not even a hint of evidence that Jesus himself was influenced by either of these two Eastern religions.

WAS JESUS INFLUENCED BY HINDUS OR BUDDHISTS?

Jesus was, of course, a Jew, but since he challenged the priesthood of the Temple, as well as many of the norms, customs, and laws of Judaism, we naturally wonder if he was influenced by philosophies and religions other than Judaism. During the time of Jesus, Judea/Palestine was rife with sectarian movements, as well as religious philosophies that had their roots in the Gentile world. So Jesus may have been influenced by any combination of those influences.

Because John the Baptist plays such an important role in the canonical Gospels, scholars have long taken it for granted that Jesus had been John's disciple prior to the beginning of his own ministry. John, however, was a messianic and apocalyptic preacher

---

7 Elaine Pagels, *The Gnostic Gospels*, New York, Vantage Press, 1989, p. xxi.

who believed the end of the world was at hand. For John, repentance was the necessary response to the coming Kingdom of God, since only the righteous would be saved.

Jesus, on the other hand, did not believe the world was about to end [8], but taught that the Kingdom of God was here and now. While John called for repentance and a change of behavior, Jesus taught that people just needed to perceive reality with new eyes. If they could alter their perception, Jesus knew, they would see that God was everywhere, most especially within themselves.

If Jesus had been a disciple of John, then the two men may have split over disagreements on such issues. In that event, they would have been teachers in competition with one another. But there is also the possibility that Jesus was never personally associated with John at all, and that the Baptist tradition was fused with the Jesus tradition after the Baptists joined the Jesus movement when John was beheaded by King Herod. It is equally possible that Baptists (who were messianists) had no association with the Jesus people either, but joined Paul's Messianist (Christian) movement years after the death of Jesus. In this event, the Christian authors of the Gospels—who wrote much later still—combined the two traditions in their mythological stories about Jesus and John.

Over the years, a host of people outside the Christian academic community have suggested that Jesus may have been an Essene, or that John was an Essene, or both. But there is no real evidence to suggest such a connection. There are some similarities between the Essenes and John, but that does not hold true for Jesus. Jesus' teachings were incompatible with those of the Essenes—or those sectaries of Qumran that people assume were Essenes.

There is evidence for yet another possibility: the canonical Gospels often referred to Jesus as "the Nazarene." The Church—and most scholars as well—have always claimed that the title, Nazarene, indicated that Jesus had come from the town of Nazareth in Galilee. But there are some scholars who now contest this assumption and suggest that there was an actual Jewish mystical sect known as the Nazarenes, and it is even possible that Jesus was the leader of this sect.

---

8 The Church has always taught otherwise, but recent work on the source Gospels of "Q" and the first layer of tradition in *The Gospel of Thomas* show that Jesus was not an apocalyptic preacher like John.

All of this is guesswork at best. We actually know almost nothing about Jesus' early influences. In the earliest narrative Gospel, *Mark*, Jesus just suddenly appears on the scene in the company of John the Baptist. Since the author of this Gospel was a Greek-speaking Gentile, probably writing from Rome some forty years after the death of Jesus, he apparently felt no need to invent an early life of Jesus. All that mattered to him was what Jesus did during the single year of his ministry.

Neither was the author of John's Gospel—written much later—compelled to invent an early history of Jesus. But the authors of *Matthew* and *Luke*, writing near the end of the first century, wanted to tie Jesus to Israel's prophetic history. To do this, they had to create fictional stories based on biblical prophecy. Those stories, like Luke's story of Jesus being presented at the Temple at age twelve, are myths, not history.

The general public, unfortunately, does not read the work of biblical scholars; therefore, the average reader has the tendency to interpret the Bible as if it were literal history. As a consequence, various people outside academia during the nineteenth century began speculating about what Jesus might have been doing during all those "missing" years (between the ages of twelve and thirty) prior to beginning his public ministry. Surely he hadn't gained all his wisdom from Judaism; he must have traveled to faraway places like India and Tibet where he studied with Hindu gurus and Buddhist lamas.

Such speculation, initially, was the result of various English and American critics of orthodox Christianity who had begun to adopt Eastern philosophy for the first time as a result of the first wave of Indian gurus coming to the West during the nineteenth century. Strongly influenced by Hinduism, new American movements such as the Theosophical Society, founded by Helena Petrovna Blavatsky in New York in 1875, began considering the possibility of a connection between Jesus and Hinduism.

Anne Besant took up the cause when Madame Blavatsky died, and the Society spawned spin-offs like the "I Am" movement founded by Guy Warren Ballard, later taken to new heights by Mark and Elizabeth Claire Prophet, who founded Summit Lighthouse. This organization, along with later movements such as the Self-Realization Fellowship founded by Paramahansa Yogananda, all had a vested interest in establishing a connection between Jesus, Hinduism, and Buddhism.

Such organizations became easy prey for charlatans who manufactured fictional stories about Jesus having traveled to India and Tibet. The best known of these stories was told by Nicolas Notovitch—a Russian Jew who converted to Greek Orthodoxy. In 1887 Notovitch wrote a book titled *The Unknown Life of Jesus Christ*, in which he included a legend about a man known as Saint Issa. As the story unfolds, it turns out that Saint Issa was really Jesus, and this Jesus had gone to Tibet to study with Buddhist lamas—or so Notovitch claimed.

Shortly after Notovitch published his book, the great Orientalist Max Muller, along with other scholars of his day, took it upon themselves to debunk Notovitch's story and expose it as a hoax—which indeed it turned out to be. For those who are interested in this drama, I have included an analysis of the whole affair in an appendix at the back of this book.

Suffice it to say that if Notovitch had known the first thing about Buddhist history, he would not have invented his Saint Issa hoax. Jesus could not have studied with Tibetan Buddhist lamas for the very simple reason that Buddhism didn't reach Tibet until *six centuries* after Jesus' death. Had Jesus gone to Tibet, he would have discovered, not Buddhists, but shamans and practitioners of Bon, the indigenous religion of Tibet—which worshiped a pantheon of spirits, and practiced animal—and sometimes human—sacrifice.

Had Jesus actually gained his wisdom from Eastern gurus, he would be a much less imposing historical and religious figure. It is Jesus' uniqueness from all other teachers that has always made him important. Jesus, while being a mystic, was not a quietist, as the Buddha and most mystics are. He was a social revolutionary as well as a spiritual one. He stood up to the hypocrisy of those who publicly made a display of their religion, and he challenged the social order—the inequities of Jewish society.

This book, however, is about similarities, not differences. And Jesus' similarities to other great religious figures, like his social criticism, probably came naturally—not as a result of being indoctrinated by wise men from the East. Consider this: If Jesus was an enlightened being—which I like to think he was—would he not have taught many of the same things that Krishna, the Buddha, and Lao Tzu did? If Jesus tapped into the

Source of Being itself, how could his teachings not have similarities to the teachings of other enlightened beings?

What impresses me the most about Jesus as a person who "woke up" is that he tried to explain his mystical insights to people who didn't have the slightest idea of what he was talking about. The Buddha was fortunate enough to "wake up" in India—the most mystically oriented culture on Earth. When people met him after his enlightenment they would say, "Congratulations, we knew you could do it!" When Jesus woke up in first century Palestine, he must have looked around at his situation and thought, "Uh-oh."

Certainly Jesus could have kept his new mystical understanding of reality to himself. Had he done so—had he just enjoyed his private bliss in the Kingdom of God—he might have lived to a ripe old age, and died a peaceful death like the historical Buddha. But Jesus was passionate and felt compelled to share his wisdom with as many other people as he could reach. This meant that he had no choice but to try and explain himself within the doctrinal and social confines of a religious culture that was completely unfamiliar with, and mostly antagonistic to, mystical insights about reality.

While Siddhartha Gautama was supported by a community of mystics, many of those who Jesus talked to thought he was either crazy, or blasphemous, or both. His own family rejected him and thought him demented. Most of Jesus' disciples, while obviously charmed by his charisma, often didn't understand what he was talking about. In the end, one of them betrayed him, another denied him, and the rest deserted him in his greatest hour of need.

Whatever Jesus' influences were, his teachings are often startlingly similar to those of the Eastern masters. Marcus Borg is one Jesus scholar today who sees those similarities clearly. In his book, *Jesus and Buddha: The Parallel Sayings*, Borg has this to say:

> . . . the cumulative product of my thinking and experience is the conclusion that Jesus and the Buddha are the two most remarkable religious figures who have ever lived. Moreover, there are striking similarities between them. I have sometimes said that if the Buddha and Jesus were to meet, neither would try to convert the other—not because they would regard such an effort as hopeless, but because they would recognize one another.

. . . Jesus and the Buddha were teachers of wisdom. Wisdom is more than ethics, even though it includes ethical teaching. The "more" consists of fundamental ways of seeing and being. Wisdom is not just about moral behavior, but about the "center." The place from which moral perception and moral behavior flow.

Jesus and Buddha were teachers of a world-subverting wisdom that undermined and challenged conventional ways of seeing and being in their time and in every time.

Their subversive wisdom was also an alternative wisdom: they taught a way or path of transformation.[9]

Another Christian who was aware of this East/West connection was the great Catholic monk and mystic, Thomas Merton. Much of his life was dedicated to finding the similarities between Western and Eastern monasticism and mysticism. He traveled extensively in Asian lands, had a special affinity for Buddhism, especially Zen, and wrote *Zen and the Birds of Appetite*. In his final work, *The Asian Journal*, Merton expressed his love for Eastern religions and expounded on the importance of the sacred Hindu text, the *Bhagavad Gita*. As for the ancient teachings of Taoism, Merton wrote his own translation of *The Tao of Chuang Tzu*.

There have also been many Hindu and Buddhist teachers who have approached the subject of commonality between Jesus' teachings and their own. One such contemporary teacher is the Vietnamese Buddhist monk, Thich Nhat Hanh, who wrote *Living Buddha, Living Christ,* and *Going Home: Jesus and Buddha as Brothers*. It is worth noting that the Introduction to *Living Buddha, Living Christ* was written by Elaine Pagels, and the Foreword by the Catholic monk, Brother David Steindl-Rast.

ONE REALITY OR TWO?

While Christianity has its failings, were it not for that religion, virtually none of Jesus' teachings would have survived. The world would never have heard of him because the early Jesus movement built around his teachings disappeared after 70 C.E. when Jerusalem was

---

9 Marcus Borg, *Jesus and Buddha: The Parallel Sayings*, Berkeley, Seastone/Ulysses Press, 1997, pp. v–vi, viii.

destroyed by the Romans, and the Jews were forced into exile in the first great Diaspora. Ironically, it was the religion *about* Jesus that preserved the religion *of* Jesus.

Jesus was not a Christian, however. Contemporary *New Testament* scholars argue that Jesus never identified himself with God, nor did he think of himself as the Messiah.[10] They insist that such notions sprang from the faith of later Christians who gradually began to think of Jesus as a divinity.

Most scholars consider Jesus' "I am" statements in *The Gospel According to John* to be the words of the Christian author, not the words of the historical Jesus. But Jesus the mystic might have said words very similar to these, and those words may have been misconstrued. Is it not possible that Jesus said something like "I and the Father are one," and meant it in the same way Krishna did?

The numerous "I am" statements from the Gnostic Gospels can only be understood properly by realizing that the speaker (or author) is merely channeling the voice of God. Certainly the Gnostic Christian who put the following words into Jesus' mouth understood Jesus this way:

> I am the Light above everything; I am the All; all came forth from me and all has returned to me. Split the wood and I am there. Lift up the stone and you will find Me there.[11]

In the *Bhagavad Gita*, Krishna teaches Arjuna, "Tat tvam Asi," "Thou art That." Atman (the Self, or soul) *is* Brahman (God). The being-ness of the individual is inextricably connected to "Being" itself. Since the essence of the individual, the Self or Atman, is divine, it is also immortal. While the physical body and one's ego-identity are subject to birth, decay, and extinction, nothing can harm the Spirit within. This Atman, this Self, is never born, thus it can never die. Jesus said much the same thing: "Fear not those who can kill the body but cannot kill the soul." (*Matthew* 10:28; *Luke* 12:4)

---

10 One reason for this is that in the two earliest "source" Gospels (the *Synoptic Sayings Source* and the earliest layer of *The Gospel of Thomas*) Jesus makes no references to himself.

11 *The Gospel of Thomas*, 77.

But, the Semitic religions—Judaism, Christianity and Islam—do not believe that we are part of God. Indeed, such an idea is the ultimate heresy. Since Jesus was a Jew, any claim that he might have made that suggested oneness with God would have been considered blasphemous. Judaism did not accept such a premise two thousand years ago, and it does not accept it today.

In modern times, the case for the Jewish rejection of monism was made clear in *I and Thou*, a book written by the Jewish philosopher Martin Buber in 1958. Buber's point of view was exactly the opposite of Krishna's. Buber insisted that there were not one, but two realities in the Universe: God, and God's creation. By their very nature, Buber argued, these two realities could never be one and the same. No part of God's creation could *become* God. And while we—part of God's creation—could have a *relationship* with God, we could come no closer to Him. I *and* Thou could never become I *am* Thou.

Monism and dualism represent two mutually exclusive, fundamentally incompatible, cosmologies. Certainly there have been mystics in Judaism, Christianity, and Islam who have experienced a personal identity with the All. But in order to avoid charges of heresy, they walked a very fine line when attempting to communicate their mystical insights within the confines of their religion's dogma. They had no choice but to hide their monistic insights within the language of dualism.

EASTERN PHILOSOPHY AND GNOSTIC CHRISTIANITY

If Jesus was not directly influenced by Eastern philosophy, there is the strong possibility that Gnostic Christianity was. Although the Gnostic Gospels are full of strange cosmologies and life-denying philosophy, it is still possible to recognize the influence of the Eastern worldview.

In the Gnostic Gospels the historical Jesus is somewhat irrelevant, just as he is for Paul, the self-proclaimed apostle of Christ. Here, Jesus is always to be thought of as the Christ, the avatar of God who came to awaken humanity from its sleep, not the flesh and blood teacher from Galilee. All the dialogue that takes place between Jesus and the disciples in the Gnostic Gospels takes place after the crucifixion. This is not the historical Jesus speaking; this is the risen Christ. Here, Jesus is more of a spiritual presence than a physical one.

Except for specific sayings in *The Gospel of Thomas*, the Gnostic Gospels do not help us understand who the historical Jesus was. The Gnostic Christ is like the Hindu Krishna in the Bhagavad Gita—a mythical avatar through whom the Godhead speaks. It is God who, time after time, in countless forms, through countless ages, reveals Himself in flesh, or in the appearance of flesh—and walks among us.

> *I am in everything. I uphold the heavens, I am the foundation which supports the planets, I am the Light that shines everywhere, that gives joy to souls. I am the life of the world: I am the sap in trees, and the sweet water that lies beneath the children of matter.*
>
> —The Manichean Psalms

> *I am the origin of all things. In me the whole universe originates and dissolves . . . All this is strung in Me, as a row of jewels on a thread. I am the wetness of water . . . the radiance in the moon and the sun . . . I am the sweet fragrance in earth, and the brilliance in fire am I: the life in all beings.*
>
> —*Bhagavad Gita*

The Gnostic Jesus teaches many of the same things that Krishna does: The world is an illusion. All created things are impermanent, so being attached to them is pointless. The purpose of life is to attain knowledge (gnosis), an experiential realization that the Self that lies within us all is truly divine substance. Atman is Brahman. The Self *is* God.

For orthodox Christianity, the human condition is due to original sin. For Gnostic Christians, the human condition—including disease and death—is due to ignorance: ignorance of one's own divine nature. Thus, the Gnostic Christ did not appear on earth to save humanity from sin and death. Christ came to dispel ignorance and illusion, and to lead those who had awakened back home to God.

Like Krishna, Christ taught that humanity's ignorance and alienation from the All was the result of attraction to, and desire for, the impermanent pleasures of the material world—something the historical Jesus taught as well. The way out of this dilemma is in renouncing the world of impermanence, dedicating one's life to the job of attaining gnosis, and unifying and purifying the Self within.

The Gnostic Christ (and the historical Jesus), like the Buddha, like Krishna, like Lao Tzu, taught that all material things are impermanent—whether they be riches, or one's own body. Attachment to that which is impermanent causes suffering. Give up attachment and suffering ceases.

Like Lao Tzu, the Gnostic Jesus taught that the created order was manifested in pairs of opposites: yin and yang, light and darkness, good and evil, life and death, love and hate, male and female. This Jesus taught that, in order to attain unity with God once more, it was necessary to unite the opposites—within and without, above and below. A single, spiritual, eye must take the place of eyes. The masculine and feminine aspects of the individual must be united into a single, androgynous, Being. According to the Gnostic interpretation of the Genesis creation story, Eve's creation from Adam's rib was a metaphor for the split within human consciousness. The Gnostic Christ taught that gnosis and inner harmony—reentry to the Garden of Eden—could only be achieved by reintegrating our masculine and feminine natures.

At least some—perhaps all—of the various schools of Gnostic Christianity believed in reincarnation. And there is no question that they all believed that the soul was immortal. But the most important parallel between Gnostic Christianity and Eastern religions is the emphasis upon attaining enlightenment in this lifetime. The great quest of Hinduism, Buddhism, and Gnostic Christianity is to seek and find the means for liberating oneself from the bonds of the material, illusory, world.

Such liberation in all traditions is not through grace, but through individual effort, and only through individual effort. While Gnostic Christians accepted the crucifixion of

Jesus, they gave no theological meaning to that terrible event— except in proposing that Jesus left his body and did not really suffer on the cross.

As for the resurrection of Jesus, Gnostic Christians considered it a spiritual, not physical, event. For the individual Christian, resurrection of the dead was not something that would take place at the end of time. Resurrection in Christ was something that took place here and now, a new state of consciousness that did not change when the physical body died.

For early "orthodox" Christianity, Gnostic Christianity was the ultimate heresy. And nothing would make an early Church father see red faster than suggesting that Jesus didn't suffer on the cross. For Eastern philosophy and for Gnostic Christianity, suffering is a limitation and something to overcome. But for Christian orthodoxy, suffering is the *point*. Mel Gibson—a Roman Catholic—made that very clear in his movie, *The Passion of the Christ*.

This raises other questions: Can we consider Gnostic Christianity a valid form of Christianity? Could it claim the right to speak for Jesus in the same way orthodoxy could? Did it have any relationship to "original" Christianity?

It is important to understand that neither form of Christianity had much to do with the historical Jesus, or the original Jesus movement that formed around him both before and immediately after his crucifixion. This movement, with its headquarters in Jerusalem, died out after 70 C.E. After this date, only Christianity existed. Early Christianity was not one movement, but many. There were virtually hundreds of early gospels, and each of them represented a different form of Christian faith. Over time, however, only two forms of Christianity survived and battled for supremacy.

The Church has always taught that Gnostic Christianity was a late heretical movement, but scholars now know better. There is evidence in Paul's letters to the Corinthians, Galatians, and Philippians that some of the Christians Paul refers to as "false apostles" preaching "false gospels" were actually Gnostic Christian missionaries. If this is true, then Gnostic Christianity developed at the very same time as Paul's supposedly "orthodox" version did.

In addition, the *New Testament* book *Acts of the Apostles* contains references to the two original founders of Gnosticism: Simon Magus and Nicolas. In *Acts*, Nicolas was one of the first seven deacons elected to run the financial affairs of the first Jesus community in Jerusalem. Simon Magus was a former magician, Christian convert, and mythological adversary of Simon Peter.

In addition to these references, there is also mention—in the form of a condemnation—of the Nicolatians (the supposedly heretical sect founded by Nicolas)—in the *New Testament Book of Revelations*. While the stories themselves probably have little historical value, they prove that both orthodox and Gnostic forms of Christianity originated at the same time.

One further piece of evidence is worthy of note: *The Gospel of Thomas* (the full text of which was discovered at Nag Hammadi in 1945) is generally considered a Gnostic Christian text. But it contains formerly unknown sayings that scholars are now certain come from the historical Jesus. It also contains *earlier versions* of sayings that have parallels in the canonical Gospels. This historical layer of *Thomas* is dated to 50 C.E., making it the earliest known Gospel, and contemporary with Paul's letters—which are dated between 50 C.E. and 65 C.E.

Besides *The Gospel of Thomas*, there are other Gnostic and apocryphal texts attributed to the disciple Thomas, and scholars believe that they all originated within a community formed around Thomas. It is interesting to note that in Church tradition, Thomas was the disciple tasked with taking the Christian Gospel to India. This tradition seems to have some historical foundation since there are still traces of a Thomas tradition in India today. It is unlikely that Thomas himself ever traveled to India, but Thomas Christians did.

Because of such new discoveries many scholars are now making the argument that Gnostic Christianity can be considered just as original and just as valid as its orthodox cousin. In fact, had it not been for the fourth century Roman emperor, Constantine—who sided with the orthodox Church and persecuted Gnostic Christians out of existence—this mystical form of Christianity might still be practiced today.

How would our society differ today had this been the case? Would society be different if our culture and religion encouraged intuitive awareness instead of intellectual analysis? Would our nation's foreign policies differ if they were based on a unified worldview instead of xenophobia and self-interest? And might our own lives be different had we been encouraged from birth to seek God consciousness instead of worshiping a distant patriarchal judge of the universe?

Up until this point we've discussed the teachings of Jesus, Buddha, Krishna, and Lao Tzu only in terms of theology and philosophy—both of which are intellectual exercises which, in themselves, are empty of reality. Now let's look at them from a mystic's vantage point—as personal aspects of our own experience.

LET ME TAKE YOU HIGHER

> . . . it is easier to sail many thousand miles through cold
> and storm and cannibals, in a government ship, with five
> hundred men and boys to assist one, than it is to explore
> the private sea, the Atlantic and Pacific Ocean of one's being alone.
>
> —Henry David Thoreau, *Walden*

While Christianity has produced its own mystics over the centuries, orthodox theologians have rarely placed any value on the contemplative life—and certainly not upon its perceptions of reality. They have somehow been able to "work around" all those teachings of Jesus that support a mystical worldview.

It doesn't seem to occur to the average theologian that his or her premises are based entirely upon intellectual concepts that are themselves a product of ordinary waking consciousness—as if this were the only valid form of consciousness. From that perspective, certainly, everything in the universe does appear to be separate and apart.

This self-imposed limitation leaves theologians with no other choice but to consider mystical insights, whether naturally or chemically induced, to be hallucinogenic. This is ironic given that mystics insist just the opposite: it is "normal" consciousness that produces an illusory world. What we know from modern science (or at least what science tells us) is that all forms of consciousness are the result of chemical interactions within the human brain. If "higher" levels of conscious—or altered states—are hallucinations, then so are our everyday thoughts!

Better living through chemistry is the order of the day. We take one pill to pump us up, another to calm us down. Overly anxious? Don't worry, we've got a pill for that. Depressed? Just take some of these and you'll feel happy again in about two weeks. Have a fear of flying? Ask the flight attendant for a couple shots of Jack Daniels and you'll love the experience.

Today, we think nothing of altering our brain chemistry in order to better cope with life. Yet our society has a taboo against doing the same thing for religious purposes. This attitude overlooks the fact that when it comes to consciousness—chemicals, the human brain, and religious experience have always gone hand in hand.

Many *New Testament* scholars, for instance, believe that the apostle Paul's out-of-body experiences were brought on by epileptic seizures—which, in turn, were brought about by chemical shifts within the brain. William James pointed out more than a century ago that even alcohol can induce mystical raptures.

Since human perception is dependent upon chemical reactions within the brain, we can never know—objectively— just what "real" reality is. We can never know, and certainly never prove, that our reality is the same as the next person's. We must, if we are honest, rephrase Descartes' famous dictum from "cogito ergo sum" to "cogito ergo sum—cogito": I think, therefore I am—I think.

For now though, critics of altered states of consciousness argue that episodes of mystical awareness are either unnaturally induced—and, therefore, invalid—or are purely accidental—which also makes them invalid. But I think it is safe to say that those who make this judgment have never taken "a trip around the head" as Timothy Leary used to put it. It's not likely that very many scientists have ever had a mystical experience, with or without drugs. As human beings, we all seem to operate on the principle that only our own experiences of reality are legitimate, while the other guy's are delusional.

Those of us who were participants in the psychedelic era of the 1960s no longer look at reality that way. Because we took the Magical Mystery Tour, most of our lives were altered dramatically as a result. No, we didn't go insane or destroy all of our brain cells. Rather—and this is just a personal opinion—we simply became more perceptive human beings.

This might not have been the case at all were it not for the fact that the psychedelic era coincided with an invasion of spiritual gurus from the East. Those who claimed that higher consciousness could be achieved *naturally* came to America at the precise moment the Counter Culture discovered marijuana, LSD, peyote, psilocybin, and mescaline. The combination of these two forces ultimately altered the face of Western religion.

During the 1950s, Western students and teachers of Eastern philosophy, such as Alan Watts, paved the way for psychologists like Richard Alpert to become Ram Dass during the 1960s. Ram Dass was able to communicate with an entire generation of spiritual seekers and make spiritual sense out of the drug-induced mystical experiences they were having, precisely because he, too, had experienced the same altered states of consciousness.

Dr. Alpert's scientific experiments with LSD at Harvard got him fired, along with Dr. Timothy Leary and Dr. Ralph Metzner. Alpert then went to India where he met his guru, Neem Karolie Baba, who gave him the spiritual name of Baba Ram Dass.

My favorite story in Ram Dass' classic first book, *Be Here Now,* was when Neem Karolie Baba asked the then Dr. Richard Alpert for some of his "medicine." Since the request was made through an interpreter, Alpert didn't understand what the guru wanted at first. Finally it became clear that the guru was asking for some LSD, which Alpert had with him. Alpert considered this an odd request, even a potentially harmful one. But the guru kept holding out his hand, so Ram Dass finally gave him a tab of the magical drug.

One serving was more than enough "acid" for a good, and usually safe, twelve hour "trip." But instead of swallowing the LSD, the guru held out his hand for more. Now Alpert really started to become apprehensive. What would happen if this guru flipped out? He would be to blame. Alpert tried to explain the situation through the interpreter, but still the guru was insistent, so Alpert gave him another dose.

Neem Karolie, however, indicated that he wanted even more. In the end, Richard Alpert gave the guru enough LSD to send him off into another universe with no return ticket. The guru smiled and popped the handful of mind-bending acid tabs into his mouth and swallowed.

Feeling extremely uncomfortable, Richard Alpert could only wait to see what would happen when the LSD (which takes about an hour to start working) took effect. An hour passed, with no change. The guru just sat there in a lotus posture and smiled ("twinkled," as Ram Dass later put it). Two hours passed, three. Still, Alpert saw no change. Neem Karolie Baba never moved from his full lotus posture, and simply continued to "twinkle."

Ram Dass' point in telling this story was simply to illustrate that Neem Karolie Baba's consciousness was so much higher than ordinary consciousness, that even a handful of mind-altering chemicals had no effect on it. The answer to expanded consciousness, Dr. Alpert suddenly understood, was *not* to be found in drugs. Richard Alpert, former professor, former Jewish psychologist, became the disciple of a guru dressed in rags—and it changed his life forever.

Many, perhaps most, of us who experimented with psychedelic drugs during that era also turned to Eastern religions for answers. Why?—because those religions are all *about* altered states of consciousness. Judaism, Christianity, and Islam teach God, but Eastern religions teach God *consciousness*. The Counter Culture needed to understand the meaning of their drug-induced experiences. Synagogues, churches, and mosques offered no answers.

> According to the drug cultists, men today are thirsting for the direct, personal experience of God—regardless of his actual nature. In other words, it matters not whether God lies within or without; in either case, men need and want a sense of direct communion with the ultimate source of their faith. The divine–human encounter is not found in church, where little or nothing is done to promote it. But it is found in LSD, the cultists believe. Thus LSD challenges the church to do as well and offer as much.[12]

It has been forty years since those words were written, and it is important to note that there is no longer an "LSD cult," if there ever was one. It did not take many young people very long to figure out that drugs were a dead end. What goes up must come down. If drugs couldn't maintain one's high, perhaps meditation and yoga could.

One did not need to have an experience of God to appreciate the value of altered states of consciousness. The first time I took LSD, I merely watched a sunset at the

---

12 William Braden, *The Private Sea: LSD and the Search for God*, Chicago, Bantam Books, 1968, p. 4.

beach in an indescribable state of bliss. A sunset over the ocean is always a beautiful sight. This was something far better.

Back at home, the usual mess left by my roommates did not bother me at all. In fact, everything looked perfect just the way it was—not an insignificant revelation for an anal-retentive personality. LSD and marijuana taught me one important lesson: reality can be perceived on many different levels. Everyday consciousness is simply the default consciousness evolution hard-wired into our brains—no doubt because it ensures our physical survival. Otherwise, it is no better or worse than any other type of consciousness.

I first recognized altered states of consciousness some years earlier—and without the aid of drugs. If the experience I had then cannot be classified as mystical, it certainly qualified for what the psychologist Abraham Maslow called a "peak experience."

I had taken a year off after my second year of college to earn enough money to continue, but also because my previous career goal had gone down the tubes. Suddenly, I hadn't the faintest idea what I should do with my life. Worse still, I was pressuring myself unmercifully to figure it out, and quickly. But after half of this year had gone by, I still didn't have a clue.

On this particular day, I was helping my parents by pulling weeds in their rose garden. My mind was dwelling on this life predicament, and I was feeling confused and rather despondent. Suddenly a voice came into my mind, saying something like, "You will serve Me for the rest of your life. You will be a minister to My people."

I experienced no burning bush. I wasn't blinded by the light. And I was fully aware that God's "voice" was coming from some deep place within myself. Even so, it overpowered me. I had never before considered studying for the ministry. The thought had never entered my mind until this very moment. I didn't think I was crazy enough to come up with an idea like this on my own, so whether it was God or my subconscious advising me, I was still incredulous.

The Voice persisted, but I told it in no uncertain terms, and in a dozen different ways, that it had the wrong guy. I wasn't smart enough. I wasn't holy enough. I wasn't devoted enough, and on and on and on. But God, my subconscious, whatever it was, countered my every argument and excuse. I felt like Jacob wrestling with an angel.

Finally, I could resist no longer and simply gave up. I surrendered to what I considered to be God's will. This complete letting go of my own will overwhelmed me with relief. I don't know how long I knelt there in the dirt, sobbing, but it was quite some time.

Finally, the tears ceased flowing, I stood up, and the world was transformed before my eyes! Everything looked glorious and new, and I felt like I had entered the Kingdom of God. Of course I knew the world was no different than before, but my perception of it had changed completely.

I was low man on the totem pole where I had been working during this year, and I had to take flak not only from the boss, but from clerks and from customers as well—a perfect situation for someone with a generally grumpy mood and a critical state of mind. But now all of those negative traits suddenly disappeared.

For the next seven days, there was nothing but love in my heart and on my lips. Absolutely nothing bothered me. I was unable to become angry or upset or depressed—not even for a moment. As a consequence, every word that came out of my mouth, every action I took, came from a place of pure love. I had been transformed. I had achieved sainthood in the blink of an eye.

When I woke up the morning of the eighth day, however, Saint Richard was gone. And for the past four decades I have grieved over the loss of him. But even though I had fallen back to Earth, I now *knew* what Jesus meant when he talked about being born anew. I knew what he meant when he spoke of the Kingdom of God. The Kingdom was not a metaphor, it was a *reality*. It was a state of conscious! Grace had allowed me to glimpse Paradise through a window. It was now up to me to find the door so that I might enter.

Many of us in modern times have taken similar journeys. Our paths have brought us together—to this very moment, when we hold in our hands some of the greatest spiritual wisdom the world has ever known. These words are more than inspiration. They are signposts along the road that will lead us back home.

The Great Way

The mountain is the mountain
And the Way is the same as of old.
Verily what is changed Is my own heart.

— Anonymous

The Way spoken of by the world's great teachers is not one single path, yet all paths lead to the same destination. Traveled by the pilgrim, the Way is the path to Life. It is the quest for our own personal holy grail. The Way stretches out before us, endless. It leads beyond the horizon, yet it begins with a single step.

Once the Way is chosen, there is no turning back. We may stop and rest awhile. We may tarry here and there for as long as necessary. We may even fall asleep by the side of the road. But we will eventually awaken no matter how long we sleep. Then, recognizing that the day's shadows are falling long across the path, we stir ourselves, cinch up our belts, and continue forward.

If we do not know where the Way begins there are those who can show us. If we become lost, there are those who can give us directions. If we need company, there are those who will be our traveling companions. But they can walk with us just so far. Eventually they must part, bidding us good journey, knowing that the path we travel is a path we must take alone.

The *New Testament* book, *Acts of the Apostles*, tells us that sometime after the death of Jesus, his friends and disciples formed a community in Jerusalem. The name of this community, *Acts* tells us, was called "the Way." This gathering of the Way was not

a Christian community, however, because Christianity had yet to be invented. Rather, the Way was the religion *of* Jesus, not the later religion *about* him.

Acts of the Apostles tells us that Saul of Tarsus, later to become Paul, the apostle of Christ, initially persecuted the Way: " . . . if he found any belonging to the Way, men or women, he might bring them bound to Jerusalem." (*Acts* 9:2). Later, the author of *Acts* has Paul say, "I persecuted the Way to death." (*Acts* 22:4).

Acts leads us to believe that Paul—once he renounced his old ways and began preaching his unique gospel of the Christ—became the friend and co-worker of the leaders of the Way in Jerusalem: James, the brother of Jesus, Simon Peter, and John. But the author of *Acts*—written around the end of the first century—was trying to rehabilitate Paul's reputation as an adversary of these men.

In the letter to his church in Galacia, Paul wrote that, three years after his "conversion," he went to Jerusalem, hoping to work hand in hand with James, Peter, and John.

But in the end, the differences between Paul and the leaders of the Way turned out to be irreconcilable. Paul finally opposed these men openly, and after he verbally attacked Peter in Antioch, the followers of the Way went one direction, and Paul's Christianity went another (Galatians 1:11–2:14).

Nevertheless, *Acts* insists that Paul himself taught "the Way" (*Acts* 19:9; 19:23). He even insists that Paul was a Nazarene like Jesus (*Acts* 24:5) and then states that the sect of the Nazarenes and the sect of "the Way" were one and the same (*Acts* 24:14).

Finally, the author of *Acts* mentions "the Way" one last time when he tells the story of Paul's trial for heresy. Antonius Felix, procurator of Judea, under whom Paul was being tried on this occasion, was himself said to have "accurate knowledge of the Way" (*Acts* 24:21), and apparently Paul didn't measure up.

While "the Way," as a designation for Jesus' particular wisdom tradition, appears in *Acts of the Apostles* seven times, these references alone are not sufficient evidence that Jesus' disciples were actually known by this name—since the name appears nowhere else in the *New Testament*. Yet Jesus *did u*se the term when describing the difficulty of the spiritual path:

Enter by the narrow gate; for the gate is wide and the
way is easy, that leads to destruction, and those who
enter by it are many. For the gate is narrow and the
way is hard, that leads to Life. And those who find it are few.

—Matthew 7:13; *Luke* 13:24

Hsin Hsin Ming, the Third Chinese Patriarch of Zen, blended Taoism with Buddhism, and his commentary on the Great Way offers a different perspective:

The Way is not difficult for those who have no preferences. When love and hate are both absent, everything becomes clear and undisguised. Make the slightest distinction, however, and heaven and earth are set infinitely apart. If you wish to see the truth, then hold no opinions for or against anything. To set up what you like against what you dislike is the disease of the mind.

This is a true statement, but there's a catch. Who among us has no preferences? Who does not discriminate? Who does not hold opinions? It takes a lifetime of spiritual work to develop the dispassion that Hsin Hsin Ming speaks of, and only a small minority of people in every age will do so. So the Zen Patriarch's statement is full of irony. He is telling us how life could be—how easy the spiritual path would be—if we no longer made distinctions between things. Jesus and Hsin Hsin Ming are saying the same thing in different ways.

For Lao Tzu and Taoism, the Way includes the meaning of "spiritual path," but implies a great deal more. Tao, the Way, is the *flow* of life. It is the "way of things." It is the force that moves in all things, permeates all things, governs all things. The Way cannot be manipulated, nor can it be resisted. It cannot even be known.

Tao will do what Tao does. As little people in the vast scheme of things, we succeed in life only when we let Tao flow through us, and around us, freely. Conversely, we make a good deal of trouble for ourselves every time we attempt to resist the ways of Tao. Can we make the wind stop blowing?

Lao Tzu tells us that we can only be happy, and the things we do can only be successful, if we *yield* to Tao—surrender to the way things are. Rather than a great tree resisting the wind, and sometimes breaking, we should become like bamboo, yielding and supple. Then the wind will flow through unhindered, and bamboo will not break. Happiness in life is the result of accepting everything just the way it is. Serenity is achieved when one no longer wishes for "something else."

The principle of the Great Way applies to the individual, but it also applies to nations. Lao Tzu tells us that any nation that resists change will eventually doom itself. Any ruler who does not govern the people according to the principles of the Way will ruin both the nation and himself. Today we say, "Go with the flow." If we want inner peace and outer harmony in society, we have to learn not to push the river.

To live in the Way, we must get out of the way. We cannot grasp the Way, so we must accept it with humility. And the more we simplify our lives—the more we bring it in alignment with Tao—the richer our lives will be.

The Buddha agreed: "If you seek to embrace the Way through the path of learning, the Way will not be understood. If you observe the Way with simplicity of heart, great indeed is the Way." Krishna says this also: "Both lust and aversion to the things of nature arise from man's lower nature. Do not come under their powers. These are enemies of the Way."

Lao Tzu often refers to Tao as the "Way of heaven." Jesus called Tao the Kingdom of heaven, or the Kingdom of God. Later orthodox Christians misunderstood Jesus' teaching about the Kingdom and believed that it was some sort of perfected world that would be ushered in at the end of time. Jesus, however, taught that the Kingdom was already here—here, there, everywhere. To recognize the Way, the Kingdom, one needs to develop eyes that see. And if we do, we will discover that the Kingdom, the Way of heaven, is not only everywhere around us, it is within us as well.

The Kingdom of God is within you and
all around you, yet you do not see it.

The Gospel of Thomas; parallels: *Luke,*
Mary, Dialogue of the Savior

Why should there be a reservoir
when there is a flood everywhere?

The Upanishads

Ask, and it will be given you.
Seek, and you will find. Knock, and
the door will be opened to you.

The Gospel According to Matthew;
parallels: *Luke, Thomas*

Listen to the Way
which is called the eternal.

The Upanishads

Judas asked Jesus, "How do we
find the Way?" Jesus answered, "By
developing love and compassion."

Dialogue of the Savior

Those who find the Way are those who
have love and forgiveness in their hearts.

The Bhagavad Gita

The Kingdom is not coming in any way
that you can observe. The Kingdom of
God is already here—within you.

The Gospel According to Luke; parallels: *Thomas, Mary*

Those who seek to find the One
without ceasing, will find the Lord
dwelling in their own hearts.

The Bhagavad Gita

The Way holds all things within Itself. Like the vastness of the universe, it lacks nothing, and nothing needs to be added to it.

The Third Chinese Patriarch of Zen

Listen carefully and faithfully to the Way—for it is mighty.

The Sutra of Forty-two Sections

No one can understand the Way unless they have pure hearts.

The Dhammapada

Before you set foot on the path, master yourself.

The Dhammapada

The Way is complete in itself. All blessings come from it, and it holds nothing back from anyone.

The Tao Te Ching

In bygone days men of wisdom honored the Way by declaring that it could be found by all who seek it.

The Tao Te Ching

The perfect man is one whose sins are forgiven. He becomes one with the Way.

The Tao Te Ching

The Way is empty, the Way is full. There is no way to describe what it is. Find it within yourselves.

The Tao Te Ching

The Way you have found is not known even
to the angels. It proceeds from the One.

Follow it.

Dialogue of the Savior

When I came among humanity I
opened the door to the Way. I showed
you the path that you must follow.
You will find it within yourselves.

Dialogue of the Savior

Enter by the narrow gate;
for the gate is wide and the way is easy
that leads to destruction,
and those who enter by it are many.
For the gate is narrow and the way is hard
that leads to life, and those
who find it are few.

The Gospel According to Matthew; parallel: Luke

I have revealed to you the most
secret doctrine . . . those who are
able to see it have seen the Light.

The Bhagavad Gita

The light that resides in the sun shines
light on all beings. It enters the Earth
as my Being, for I nourish all things.

The Bhagavad Gita

There are two paths that are eternal:
the path of light and the path of darkness.
One path leads to liberation,
the other leads to sorrow.

The Bhagavad Gita

Words cannot describe what the
Way is, but do not lose sight of it,
for then it might be lost forever.

The Buddha

The secret of the Way waits for those
who have overcome desire.

The Tao Te Ching

Those with a pure heart, and who
seek the Way without ceasing, will find it.
It is like cleaning glass
until the dust is removed.

The Dhammapada

I seek to understand and walk the Way,
so that I do not lose sight of it. The Way
is not complex, nor is it hidden from
anyone. People just choose to ignore it.

The Tao Te Ching

Once you have crossed the river,
leave the raft behind. This is the
Way I have taught you.

The Majjhima Nikaya Sutra

The Way is mighty, yet people
prefer smaller paths.

The Tao Te Ching

Open the door to the Way that is within you,
so that you may be a guide to those
who wish to follow you. Encourage
all those who are ready to follow the
Way and receive its blessings.

The Second Apocalypse of James

God allowed man to look outward,
but in seeing the outer, the inner is ignored.
Those who see the eternal,
turn their gaze within.

The Katha Upanishad

The Kingdom is within you, and one
who knows himself will find it.

Papyrus Oxyrhynchus; parallels: *Thomas,
Luke, Mary, Dialogue of the Savior*

When the mind becomes still,
when thinking ceases, this is
the beginning of the supreme path.

The Katha Upanishad

I am a beacon of light to those who see Me.
I am a mirror to those who look for Me.
I am a door to those who knock on
Me. I am a Way for you, the traveler.

The Hymn of Jesus from *The Acts of John*

I am the Way for the traveler.
I am the Master who watches in silence.
I am your friend and your shelter.
I am the beginning and the
end of all things.
I am the seed of the Universe.
I am the supreme treasure.

The Bhagavad Gita

Seeking within, you will find stillness.
Here there is no more fear or
attachment—only joy.

The Dhammapada

He who knows the Way does not let it
show. Neither does he seek to be rewarded
by anyone. Those who know the Way
find their reward within themselves.

The Tao Te Ching

It is good to practice the Way,
and to seek truth. Being in harmony
with the Way is even better.

The Kevaddha Sutra

Those who say they have found the
Way, have not. That which is eternal,
cannot be spoken of. It lies within.

The Tao Te Ching

Those are fortunate who have eyes
to see the great Way. They know that
there is no other path to purifying
the intellect. Seek this Way.

The Dhammapada

When the wise man hears of the Way,
he tries hard to follow it. When the average
person hears of the Way, he tries to keep it,
but eventually loses it. When those who are
ignorant hear of the Way, they just laugh.
If people didn't laugh at it,
it wouldn't be the Way.

The Tao Te Ching

Follow Me and leave the dead
to bury the dead.

The Gospel According to Matthew; parallel: Luke

Many are the paths of men, though all those
paths end in Me for those who love Me.

The Bhagavad Gita

It is easier for a camel to pass through
the eye of a needle than for a rich man
to enter the Kingdom of heaven.

The Gospel According to Matthew; parallel: Luke

The Way of the transcendent is
difficult for mortals to attain.

The Bhagavad Gita

Hurry, now, to follow the Way, for it is
plain to seek but hard to walk upon.

The Epistula Apostolorum

Let those who are wise seek the Way.
Those who find it will not return.

The Bhagavad Gita

True humanity is within you.
Seek and you will find it.

The Gospel of Mary [Magdelene]*;
parallels: Thomas, Matthew, Luke*

Follow the way of righteousness,
for it leads to the highest goal.

The Bhagavad Gita

Those who follow the Way are like dry grass. They need to be protected from the flames of desire.

The Sutra of Forty-two Sections

Act in harmony with the Way, and you will become the Way. Nurture the Way within yourself, and you will live a virtuous life.

The Tao Te Ching

It is hard for those with power and wealth to follow the Way.

The Kavaddha Sutra

The Way rewards those who embrace it. Misfortune waits for those who abandon it.

The Tao Te Ching

To live according to the Way is not easy or hard. But it is impossible for those who are fearful and lack commitment.

The Third Chinese Patriarch of Zen

If you seek the Way through learning, you will not understand it. If you seek the Way with a humble heart, then you will find it.

The Tao Te Ching

To follow the Way is goodness. To conform to the Way is greatness.

The Sutra of Forty-two Sections

To have knowledge of the Way is good. Conforming to the Way is best.

The Tao Te Ching

Value only those things in life which are eternal. Search for these things within yourself. Let everything you say come from the harmony that is within you. For I tell you, the living God is within you, and you are in Him.

Dialogue of the Savior

Do not seek deliverance because others persuade you. Let your motivation come from that which is already within you.

Dialogue of the Savior

When you perceive those things outside of you as the same as those things within you, and when you unify the male with the female within you, then you will enter the Kingdom of heaven.

The (Second) *Apocalypse of James*

Attachment and aversion to objects is natural. But do not let either have power over you. These states of mind are enemies of the Way.

The Bhagavad Gita

Following the Way is to be non-attached to worldly things. You will be in harmony with the Way when you no longer see the difference between sorrow and good fortune.

The Bhagavad Gita

Those who seek union with the Way, no longer live in delusion. Therefore, leave delusion behind and become one with the One.

The Bhagavad Gita

One who reinforces the ego by seeking
fame, while ignoring the Way, is
pursuing that which does not exist.

The Sutra of Forty-two Sections

Seeking things of the world will
result in disaster. The Way of heaven
is to retire from the world.

The Tao Te Ching

The Way is perfect. The knowledge
of One-ness brings serenity.

The Third Patriarch of Zen

The Way is empty; it cannot be filled up. It
is like a vast lake that never becomes dry.

The Tao Te Ching

It is impossible to follow the way
if you believe in dualism.

The Sutra of Forty-two Sections

The Way can be compared to a raging
river that rushes to the sea.

The Tao Te Ching

If you think the Kingdom of God is above you, then birds will find it first.

If you think it is in the ocean, then fish will discover it before you do.

Look . . . the Kingdom of God is within you and all around you.

The Gospel of Thomas; parallels: *Matthew, Luke*

With one's heart focused on yoga [union] and recognizing all things as equal, then you will see the Self within—and within all beings.

The Bhagavad Gita

The Way is not in the sky;
the Way is in the heart.

The Buddha

One can know the world without
ever leaving home. The Way can be
recognized without a window.

The Tao Te Ching

God, Tao, and Universal Mind

*Vedanta says there is nothing that is
not God . . . the living God is
within you . . . the only God to worship is the
human soul in the human body.*

—Swami Vivekananda

Buddhism, many have said, is not so much a religion as it is a psychology. It is concerned with the workings of the human mind. Its business is helping people to "wake up," to provide the tools that allow one to expand their perception of reality. Buddhism may have all the trappings of a religion—robes, altars, incense, ritual—but even though it sometimes speaks of "Universal Mind," Buddhism does not posit the existence of God. Consequently, Buddhism has no theology—no "words about God." Does God exist? The Buddhist is likely to answer, "It really doesn't matter one way or another since the human predicament remains the same in either case. Our job is to dispel illusion and alleviate suffering."

Hindus would agree with Buddhists on this point—and it's useful to remember that Buddhism began as a Hindu sect—but when Hindus describe the process of enlightenment or "waking up," they are more likely to describe their experience of "Samadhi," or bliss consciousness, as being in the presence of God. Christians of all stripes—even mystics—also consider "God consciousness" as the goal of their inner quest.

Taoism represents yet another point of view. Tao is the force that permeates heaven and earth. Its ways can be known, but not Tao itself. An ancient Taoist would probably tell us that further speculation about the "divine" nature of Tao would prove to be a waste of time.

Tao is an impersonal force in the universe, just like Universal Mind. But, then, so is "God" in most, if not all, mystical traditions, including Hinduism and Gnostic Christianity. Whatever word a mystic uses to describe Ultimate Reality, he or she is rarely speaking of a transcendent Being who created the Universe and micro-manages it.

Hinduism and Gnostic Christianity (and perhaps mystical Christianity in general) use the word "God" to describe a reality that, when examined closely, is far closer to the Universal Mind of Buddhism and the Tao of Taoism than it is to the personal God of Judaeo-Christianity and Islam.

Hindus, however, have no trouble at all personalizing the impersonal God. Their religion abounds with gods and goddesses. But this pantheon of deities—at least among the mystics of India—represents God's attributes, not individual deities. Those who developed Hinduism's pantheon of gods and goddesses many thousands of years ago were probably true polytheists. Over time, however, Hinduism evolved until it reached its greatest expression in the monistic philosophy of Vedanta, as expressed in its greatest scriptures, the *Upanishads* and the *Bhagavad Gita*.

Being all things to all people, Hinduism never found the need to renounce its gods and goddesses. Even today many Hindus continue to worship their deities as they have for thousands of years. Even mystics do not find a dichotomy here, since Hinduism has always been tolerant of all expressions of religious faith. God can be one and many simultaneously.

Buddhism developed in the opposite direction. It began as a movement without deities of any kind, and only later took on all the trappings of religion. Originally, Buddhism was quite simple and straightforward, but the Mahayana—the "Great Vehicle"—school of Buddhism eventually evolved to accommodate, not just monks who were committed to renouncing the world, but also common people who carried on the usual affairs of daily life. With this change came a cosmos of deities over time. Had Buddhism not evolved in this manner, it may well have remained just one more Hindu sect, or perhaps perished altogether.

Today, many Buddhists worship the historical Buddha much as Christians worship Christ: as a world savior (but not as God). In addition, they give devotion to many other quasi-divine figures as well. Buddhism adopted and adapted as it moved out from India into the wider Asian world. In China, it absorbed philosophical Taoism, and reinvented itself as Zen Buddhism. When Buddhism came to Tibet in the seventh century C.E., it absorbed the indigenous religion of Bon, including its pantheon of deities and demons—which exist, but only in the world of appearance.

Gnosticism was such a diverse and complex religion that it is almost impossible to generalize about its theology. Gnostic Christianity, as a religion in itself, adopted many Gnostic ideas and rejected others, while giving it a unique Christian identity. In this, it was similar to Hinduism and Buddhism in adopting a cosmos full of demons and demigods. What set it apart from those religions, however, was the insistence that the various "powers" in the Universe conspired to keep humanity ignorant of its true divine origins.

Early "orthodox" Christians were abhorred by the Gnostic expression of Christian faith, especially its cosmos of evil forces that included the Hebrew creator-god, Yahweh. Yahweh, in this case, was a demi-god unworthy of worship, and one who played the part of a dungeon master by enslaving the divine soul in a prison of flesh.

Still, one has to wonder to what degree Gnostic Christians literalized such powers, and to what degree they understood them as metaphors. Orthodox Christianity has always criticized Gnosticism in all of its forms as extreme "dualism," because it spoke of the true God as an "alien" force that exists far beyond the world of matter, and the human soul as a reality apart from the physical body.

Yet the concept of the soul in Gnosticism is little different from the concept of the immortal soul in Greek philosophy. Furthermore, for Gnostics, the world of matter didn't really exist apart from the All, the Godhead. Its separateness was merely "apparent." Ultimately, all things resolved themselves back into the All, and the Gnostic goal of joining the Self with the Godhead was, practically speaking, little different from the Hindu concept of Atman/Brahman. Ultimately, Hinduism, Buddhism, Taoism, and Gnostic Christianity all teach that there is only one single Reality in the Universe, and nothing exists apart from It. In the end, the name we give this Reality—God, Brahman, Universal Mind, Tao, or the All—is unimportant.

In the beginning the Word was moving
toward God, and God was the Word.

This one existed in God from the beginning.
Through Him all things came into being.

Without Him, nothing has come into
existence. In Him was life, and the
life was the light of humanity. The
light shines in the darkness, and the
darkness has not overtaken it.

The Gospel According to John

Once, all was darkness.
The All remained unseen within the
darkness—unknown and unknowable,
as if in a deep sleep.
Then the All became manifest as the Lord—
who alone exists, and who is self-existent.
He is everywhere.
There is no place where He is not. He
exists in all things, and all things exist in
Him. He manifests Himself from Himself.

The Ordinances of Manu

Before That-Which-Is became visible,
All things existed in Him. He holds all things
within Himself, but nothing holds Him.

The Sophia of Jesus Christ

Before He manifested Himself, he
existed within Himself. Out of Himself
He manifested all things. He is known
as the One who alone exists.

The Taittirya Upanishad

Universal Mind is like a vast ocean.
On its surface, waves disturb its
tranquility, but beneath, all is serene
and unmoved. Having no personality,
all things exist in It. But due to the
disturbance on its surface, Universal Mind
became an actor playing many parts.

The Lankavatara Sutra

In the beginning there was only Void.
Within the Void was the One.
The One is without form.
It has no features.
But within it all things exist.

Chuang Tzu

The Lord Buddha cannot be seen in visible
form, nor can he be heard in audible sound.
Those who lead evil lives cannot
perceive the Blessed One.

The Diamond Sutra

The Great Tao [Way]
pervades all things,
and causes all things
to come into existence.

The Tao Te Ching

The One is invisible, imperishable and un-nameable. It is not a god. Nothing exists above It, and nothing existed before It. It is Unity and cannot be differentiated. It is the Father of All and It exists above the All. It is the Light in which no eye can look. It is beyond perfection. It exists outside of time. It is without qualities and it contains all qualities. It is eternal, and It alone exists.

The Apocryphon of John

The Word was made flesh, and It dwelled among us.

The Gospel According to John

The One has no limits. It is neither form, nor not-form. It is indivisible. Everything that exists, exists in It. It seeks only Itself. It is eternal and the giver of eternity. It is pure Light. It is the Blessed One that never changes.

The Apocryphon of John

I Am the soul that exists in everything. I Am the beginning, middle and end of all lives. I Am the Mind dwelling in all things. I Am Light. I Am consciousness. I Am the eternal Word. I Am the One who never changes. I Am the master over the future, and Lord of death. I am in all things, and nothing moves without Me.

The Bhagavad Gita

All things manifest are filled with God. All things that are invisible are filled with God. All things flow from God, yet He does not change.

The Isha Upanishad

The visible universe came forth from Me. I am invisible, yet the source of all things. At the end of time, all things will return to Me.

The Bhagavad Gita

Ultimate Reality is immovable,
but is the cause of movement.
Only through great insight will one
comprehend this such-ness.

A manual on Zen Buddhism

Before heaven and earth came into
existence, there was only the One
which never changes. It exists in sacred
silence, and It is unaffected by actions.
It holds all things in its loving embrace,
but asks nothing for Itself. What do I
call this nameless One? I call it Tao.

The Tao Te Ching

All things are in Nirvana, and it has
been so since the beginning.

The Lankavatara Sutra

Since the beginning It has taken on
an endless series of names. I do not
know its beginning or its nature,
but I understand It through Tao.

The Tao Te Ching

All living beings—every creature, whether
from eggs or wombs, or from water,
everything manifest or un-manifest,
whether thinking or unthinking, or beyond
thought—all these come from Me, so
that all beings may reach Nirvana.

The Diamond Sutra

All things exist in pairs of opposites, being
dependent upon each other.
This cannot exist without That.
What is the power behind all this? I
recognize its presence in all things,
yet I cannot see its form.

Chuang Tzu

The Spirit flowed from It like the water of life and Light. It alone understood Its own Image. This One filled with blinding Light is pure Mind.

The Apocryphon of John

The Lord dwells in the heart of all things. He is the only reality, so don't be deceived by appearances.

The Isha Upanishad

From the beginning of time He has appeared. He has taken on many forms. He has been called by many names. In the end, He will return to Himself.

The Kerygma Petri

The One who was breathless, breathed through His own nature, apart from which nothing exists. The breath gave life to the seed of the universe which is Spirit.

The Rig Veda

The Father willed that all of creation return to Him.

Untitled Apocalypse

Through endless cycles of time, I have resolved all things in Me. Yet I do none of this. I am the Watcher who watches the drama unfold.

The Bhagavad Gita

Above the One there is nothing. He is nameless. He sees only Himself everywhere. We cannot comprehend Him, for He has no images.

The Sophia of Jesus Christ

The Lord of the Universe is limitless. He sees only Himself everywhere. His attributes are countless, and His attributes are without beginning or end.

The Bhagavad Gita

Universal Mind is perfection
without images. It is far beyond
the world of thought.
Divine Mind is undisturbed
and exists eternally.

The Lankavatara Sutra

One intrinsic Unity enfolds
all manifestations.

The Surangama Sutra

Universal Mind holds within itself
all thoughts and all actions. So it has
been since the beginning of time.

The Lankavatara Sutra

It exists everywhere, but the beginner
cannot see Its essential nature.

The Surangama Sutra

The origin of heaven and earth is
beyond the realm of thought. The Tao
that can be expressed in words is not
the everlasting Tao. This origin of all
things is revealed within ourselves.
This is the mystery of all mysteries.

The Tao Te Ching

Tao gave birth to the One.
The One gave birth to the two,
which gave birth to the three.
From the three arose all creation.

The Tao Te Ching

The nature of Tao is to return to its
own origin. Having given birth to all
things, nothing gave birth to It.

The Tao Te Ching

The Tao is a mystery. You cannot
see Its coming or going.

The Tao Te Ching

The Blessed One knows only Himself. He never changes, and has no imperfections.

The Sophia of Jesus Christ

God is Spirit, and those who worship Him, worship Him in spirit.

The Gospel According to John

The All is beyond all limitations. It cannot be comprehended with the human mind. It cannot be measured by any rule. It cannot be seen or talked about. It has no name.

The Apocryphon of John

The All encompasses all with love, so that all things that come from Him may become Him.

The Tripartite Tractate

The Lord cannot be perceived with the rational mind. He is beyond all thought, even though He resides within every being.

The Mundaka Upanishad

The force that pervades all nature, actions, and humanity is God. Those who realize this become immortal.

The Kena Upanishad

God pervades all that exists in the universe. Above and below, there is only this One.

The Bhagavad Gita

The formless Being which is beyond all things arises in all things, and never perishes.

The Mundaka Upanishad

Divine Mind is eternal. It contains
within itself all reality and all truth.

The Lankavatara Sutra

All things conform to their own
natures. Tao conforms to Itself.

The Tao Te Ching

Universal Mind is not subject to birth and
death. It is beyond all concepts of duality.

The Lankavatara Sutra

Tao is beyond all words. It can only
be comprehended in silence.

Chuang Tzu

Universal Mind is beyond all limitations.
Its essential nature is pure, free of
faults, and unaffected by individuation.
It is beyond impermanence,
distinctions, desires, and aversions.

The Lankavatara Sutra

Tao is the common ancestor of all. But
I do not know whose child It is.

The Tao Te Ching

The intrinsic Unity of All things
contains all things.

The Surangama Sutra

The Tao never answers with words. It
does not reach out for things, but all
things come to It. The unspoken plan
unfolds slowly. It gathers all things as
if in a net, so that nothing is lost.

The Tao Te Ching

All that you see is what I revealed to you.
What I am, I alone know. Behold everything
through Me, so that you may understand
what I am. For you belong to Me.

The Acts of John

From Me alone comes knowledge
and ignorance, enlightenment and
darkness, happiness and misery, life
and death, fear and fearlessness.

The Bhagavad Gita

All forms, all beings in the Universe exist
within and in relationship to each other.
In the end, all things will return
to their essential nature.

The Gospel of Mary [Magdalene]

Salt exists in water, and we can taste
each. The One which is without
end, consisting only of Awareness,
comes out of such elements, then
disappears within them once again.

The Upanishads

If you think that the Tathagata [the Great Buddha] comes or goes, sits or lays down, you have not understood what I have been teaching you. He is called the Tathagata because he is nowhere and no-when.

The Diamond Sutra

All things exist in relationship to everything else. Whether manifest or un-manifest, they come and go in relationship to everything else.

The Lankavatara Sutra

How can the Tao be named? It is no-thing. It is without cause and without effect. Tao points to itself. No name can define it.

The Tao Te Ching

It comes, it goes. Without form, it cannot be embraced. Without sound, ears cannot hear it. Without form, no one can see it.

The Tao Te Ching

Being One:
Mind, Meditation and Yoga

If the chimney is full of smoke, how can the light be seen?
If the mind is full of dirt, how can the soul shine?

—Yogaswami

The goal of all mystical paths is to recognize oneness with God, or whatever one chooses to call Ultimate Reality. We are told by spiritual teachers that we already *are* One, we just don't realize it. In reality, there is nothing to achieve, nothing to become, nothing to do but . . . wake up. And to wake up, all we have to do is change how we perceive reality. This will allow us to become aware of our essential unity with All-That-Is. But this "all we have to do" job can take a lifetime or, much more likely, many lifetimes.

Only a handful of people in any age ever fully realize this ultimate state of awareness. And most of the few who have attained this state of being have done so only after a lifetime of arduous spiritual effort. We might well wonder, then, if we already *are* One, why is it so difficult to realize it?

In a sense, the answer to that question is in the very fact that we asked the question in the first place. We use our "rational" mind to seek an answer to something that can only be recognized by our super-rational mind. Our mind, it turns out, is both the problem and the solution.

While our rational mind can do many amazing things, and is very useful and necessary in the phenomenal world, when it comes to realizing God consciousness, our thinking, questioning, debating, pondering mind gets us nowhere at all. All our mind does is steer us into a spiritual cul-de-sac.

But now that we've identified the problem, the solution seems pretty obvious and simple: just stop thinking—just power down our discursive mind so that "Essential Mind" can take over and, bingo, instant Buddha, instant Christ. If only!

The reality is that our minds are completely out of control. The human mind has often been compared to a hyper-active chattering monkey that refuses to stop moving or shut up. Anyone who has ever tried to meditate knows just how appropriate that metaphor is. Still, it would appear that we have no choice but to train our mind as if it were a new puppy that hasn't been housebroken yet. We need to become the master of our mind, not its slave.

Original man had one original
mind. It was unified.

Dialogue of the Savior

To attain the One, one's mind must
be in harmony with itself.

The Katha Upanishad

Learn to see what is right in front of you,
then you will be able to see that which is
invisible. Nothing is ever truly hidden.

The Gospel of Thomas; parallels: *Matthew, Luke*

That which is real is always real. That which
is unreal is always unreal. The person
who knows Truth, knows the difference.

The Bhagavad Gita

I saw the Lord in a vision, and my vision
did not falter. The Lord said to me, "It is
fortunate that you were able to hold this
vision of Me in your mind without losing
it; for the mind holds the treasure."

The Gospel of Mary [Magdalene]

The Self, which is God, dwells in every
being, but only those with wisdom and
perception—having the ability to hold the
mind steady—will recognize this. When the
senses obey the mind, God will be revealed.

The Katha Upanishad

I said to the Lord, "Is it through our soul or
our spirit that we are able to see visions?'
"He said to me, 'Neither. Visions
are produced by the mind."

The Gospel of Mary [Magdalene]

When the mind is controlled by
concentration and one comes to see the
self as the Self, the yogi experiences infinite
bliss. To purify the intellect is to transcend
the senses, and to transcend the senses is to
remain in bliss consciousness permanently.

The Bhagavad Gita

The sky has no east or west, nor does not make any distinctions between this and that. Distinctions arise from the human mind alone.

The Buddha

The past does not exist. The future does not exist. One should concentrate the mind on the present moment.

The Buddha

Our lives are products of our mind. What we are today is a result of what we thought yesterday. What we think today influences what happens to us tomorrow. Our entire lives are products of our mind.

The Dhammapada

The discriminating mind is like a magician who sees the world as his stage. The intuitive mind travels with the magician, becoming a mirror which reflects emptiness and impermanence.

The Lankavatara Sutra

That which fuels the fire consumes itself.

Chuang Tzu

Tao can only be understood in the present moment.

The Tao Te Ching

Recognize what is simple. Keep what is essential.

The Tao Te Ching

He who says he knows, knows not. He who truly knows, says nothing at all. For the good of the world, correct this confusion and unite all things as one whole.

The Tao Te Ching

Light comes through the mind and illuminates the whole body. When all things within you are integrated, your light will shine everywhere.

Dialogue of the Savior

When the light within is sheltered from the wind, the yogi who is perfect in concentration realizes the Self. He is then a lamp that does not flicker.

The Bhagavad Gita

Unless one is born anew, he can not see the Kingdom of God.

The Gospel According to John

Even though born in truth, all things will die. But out of death comes Life.

The Bhagavad Gita

Make everything within you harmonious.

Dialogue of the Savior

See Me in all things. Dwell in Me as I dwell in you.

The Bhagavad Gita

When you pray, enter your hidden chamber and shut the door.

The Gospel According to Matthew; parallel: *Thomas*

Shut out the physical world. Control the mind. Then you will become free.

The Bhagavad Gita

If one acts from the purity of the mind, joy will be the result. Joy will follow that person like a shadow.

The Dhammapada

In order to eliminate the discriminating mind, there must be a complete "turning around" of one's being at the deepest level of consciousness.

The Lankavatara Sutra

Eliminate the discriminating mind, so that all that remains is Universal Mind.

The Lankavatara Sutra

Meditate deeply.

The Dhammapada

Unify spirit and soul and inner harmony will follow.

The Tao Te Ching

Achieve the state of a new-born child. Clear and purify inner vision.

The Tao Te Ching

Bending like a tree in the wind, one becomes whole. When one becomes whole, all things come to a person naturally.

The Tao Te Ching

Close the door and shut out the senses. Do this and you will never be exhausted.

The Tao Te Ching

Become aware of Me within you. Focus your attention on Me, that I may become manifest in you.	Think on me in the serenity of your heart. Control your mind and become fearless. Have Me as your supreme goal.
The [Second] *Apocalypse of James*	*The Bhagavad Gita*
Find a place of stillness within yourself.	With a quiet mind, seek harmony within yourself.
The Gospel of Thomas	*The Bhagavad Gita*
See Me in yourselves, as you would see yourself in water or a mirror.	See in this body of Mine the existence of the whole universe. Be centered in the One.
Agrapha	*The Bhagavad Gita*
Meditate on Me, for all those who seek Me will find Me. Hear Me— you who have ears to hear.	Center your heart on Me. Be resolute and content. Still the mind, control the passions, and you will become dear to Me.
The Thunder: Perfect Mind	*The Bhagavad Gita*

With earnest meditation, purity of mind, and compassionate acts of kindness, you will become an island of serenity which even the greatest floods cannot sweep away.

The Dhammapada

When the subject becomes still, objects will cease to be.

A manual on Zen Buddhism

All beings long to return to the source of their origin, where perfect unity abides. There are many ways to accomplish this.

The Surangama Sutra

To reach the farthest shore, let go of all things. When your mind is free, you will travel beyond life and death.

The Dhammapada

Wise are they who center their hearts on the inner essence of things, not on outer appearances.

The Tao Te Ching

Recognize the ultimate emptiness of things. Steady yourself in stillness and achieve inner peace.

The Tao Te Ching

See the Essence behind the essence, and you will become free of fear and evil. Then you will be at peace with yourself.

The Tao Te Ching

As I travel on this path of Tao, I know of nothing else. This Way is straight and smooth, but most people choose lesser paths.

The Tao Te Ching

He who receives nourishment from
Me, will become as I Am. That
which is hidden will be revealed.

The Gospel of Thomas

Remember Me at all times, and
you will come to Me.

The Bhagavad Gita

You who have waited for Me, receive
Me. Do not be ignorant of Me,
but take Me into your heart.

The Thunder: Perfect Mind

See Me in all things. Do not become
separated from Me. I dwell in all beings.

The Bhagavad Gita

The chosen ones are those who
are one within themselves. They
will enter the Kingdom.

The Gospel of Thomas

Resting serenely in the Self, and with a
controlled mind, all desires pass away.

The Bhagavad Gita

Recognize yourself in Me. Recognize Me by
my actions. Keep these mysteries in silence.

The Hymn of Jesus from *The Acts of John*

Focus on Me, take refuge in Me, practice
yoga, and you will know Me fully.

The Bhagavad Gita

In deep meditation, taste the nectar of the dharma. Become free of sin and fear.

The Dhammapada

Some supposed they saw me as form. Others followed my voice. These are useless efforts. No one saw me at all.

The Diamond Sutra

Be alone and still within yourselves, Have no selfish desires, and the ego disappears. This is true joy.

The Dhammapada

Meditate to control the senses. Do what must be done, and suffering ceases.

The Dhammapada

With minds free of thought, serenity is discovered.

The Tao Te Ching

The origin of the world is called the Mother. To know the Mother, hold onto the child. Know the child and you will know the Mother. With such understanding you will never die.

The Tao Te Ching

While the world is full of wondrous sights, inner peace comes from staying at home.

The Tao Te Ching

It is the way of Tao to return to Itself. Its apparent weakness results from its usefulness. All things come from Tao, but Tao comes from nothing.

The Tao Te Ching

When you unify both halves of yourself, you will become as you were originally created. Then if you say to the mountain, "move," it will move.	He can be found as spokes of a wheel. As the wheel turns, He will reveal himself to you. Therefore, meditate on Him and you will reach the farthest shore which is beyond all darkness.
The Gospel of Thomas; parallels: *Matthew* and *Luke*	*The Upanishads*
Take my yoke upon yourselves, for I am a gentle master. Come to Me and you will find peace.	The yogi who is absorbed in Me will become tranquil of mind. Subdue the senses and become quiet. Let go of thinking.
The Gospel of Thomas; parallel: *Matthew*	*The Bhagavad Gita*
I will reveal all things that are hidden from you so that through perfect knowledge you will become one with Me. Reach out and grasp Me.	Let go of the intellectual mind, and concentrate your mind on Me. Step by step you will attain quietness. Give up thinking.
The [Second] *Apocalypse of James*	*The Bhagavad Gita*

If you wish to reach the farthest shore,
follow the path of dharma. Crossing over,
you will be beyond the reach of death.

The Dhammapada

To be one with Tao is to reach eternity. To
reach eternity is to reach safe haven.
To be in a safe haven is to become
whole. Then even death ceases
to hold power over you.

The Tao Te Ching

Follow the dharma and receive ultimate
bliss. Take refuge in the spiritual life.

The Anguttara Nikaya Sutra

Fish lose themselves in water.
People can lose themselves in Tao.

Chuang Tzu

Be eager to attain the attainable. Master
that which can be mastered. Realize
that which can be realized. Then
your spiritual work will bear fruit.

The Samyutta Nikaya Sutra

How do I know the world? Its
knowledge comes from within.

The Tao Te Ching

The Self

How shall I grasp it? Do not grasp it.
That which remains when there is
no more grasping is the Self.

—Panchadasi

When most of us use the word, "self," we are usually referring to our ego identity—that persona, or mask, we wear to maintain our illusion of individuality. This small self includes our subconscious mind, our intuitive mind, and virtually everything else our brains produce that make us believe we are separate and apart from every other thing in the universe.

Krishna, Plato, and Jesus, however, meant something entirely different when they used this word "self." Self, to them, refers to what lies beneath individuality. This Self is the core essence of what (not who) we really are: God, the Tao, Universal Mind. Self is what remains when the little self dies. Self is what we discover when we are "born again." Self is what appears when we cleanse our windows of perception. Self is what we recognize when we "wake up." Self, really, is all that exists.

This Self, in Hinduism, is called *Atman*. And Atman, Krishna tells us in the *Bhagavad Gita*, is Brahman, or God. The only distinction between Atman and Brahman—between Self and God—is the distinction we make ourselves. Remove that distinction and all that remains is God, or Universal Mind, or Tao.

Gnostics often referred to Self as a "spark," and God as the divine Light from which the spark emanated. For them, individual sparks of divine Light had broken off from the Godhead, and were trapped within, and by, the human body. In our ignorance, humans are unaware that this spark of Light exists within us. But when we become aware of our true nature, the Self, we dissolve back into the Divine Light.

Unlike Hindus and Gnostic Christians, Buddhists rarely speak of Self in the same way Jesus and Krishna do. In fact, much Buddhist teaching emphasizes "not-Self." Although pursuing much the same course toward enlightenment, the Buddha often turned the mind back on itself through the process of negation: "not this, not that." This process forces the disciple to give up all thought patterns by exhausting them, as in Zen Buddhist training. The closest concept to Self in Buddhism is "Mind"—not the intellectual mind, but what stands behind it. Inasmuch as there is a section in the book on Mind, we will leave these teachings for later.

Neither did ancient Taoism emphasize the concept of Self. While not denying it, Taoists of old simply emphasized the reality of Tao alone. Perhaps the Taoist masters decided that giving name to something other than Tao would be too misleading, and give rise to too much philosophy. After all, when one's sense of individuality disappears, there is nothing left but Tao. Buddhists might add the comment that ego is an illusion, and Tao was all that ever existed in the first place.

But what precipitates the ego's disappearance? What causes the thinking mind to cease its thinking? Lao Tzu might say that any attempt to answer such questions would require too much activity of the discriminating mind. Better to just shrug one's shoulders and laugh.

In order to know everything you must
first know yourself. If you do not know
yourself, Then you know nothing. Those
who know themselves also know the All.

The Gospel of Thomas

If you would become perfect,
discover the Self within. Seek this
awareness, not intelligence.

The Bhagavad Gita

A person who only sees his external
self, rather than the Self within,
not only diminishes himself, but
misleads others as well.

The Gospel of Mani

The Self resides in all beings, but it is only
recognizable to those with intuitive abilities.

The Upanishads

Those who have truly found the Self within
recognize that it exists everywhere.

Dialogue of the Savior

All those who devote themselves to
the Self within make it an object of
devotion that can never perish.

The Upanishads

Do you not understand that what
you see is what you will become?
Therefore seek the Self within yourself,
because this is who you really are.

Dialogue of the Savior

Recognizing the Lord everywhere
reflects the Self within.
This is the eternal reward.

The Bhagavad Gita

In the realms of Suchness there is neither "self" nor "other." The only way to see what is real is to consider all things as being "not two."

Seng-Ts'an

Wisdom comes from knowing oneself. He who knows himself is enlightened.

The Tao Te Ching

When Mind is seen as all minds, there are no more words. In this understanding exists past, present and future.

Seng-Ts'an

Some people recognize the Self and are amazed. Other people who hear of the Self just wonder. Still others don't understand at all.

The Tao Te Ching

Everyone has recognized the Self—one's essential nature. But few have realized it.

The Surangama Sutra

Strip away the non-essential, and the essential will reveal itself.

The Tao Te Ching

Recognizing the unity of all life, one sees his own Self in all other beings. This allows one to be impartial about all things.

The Buddha

The Self that is restrained in all things will never suffer. It will endure forever.

The Tao Te Ching

Your salvation comes from being aware of
what is already inside of you.
If you are unaware, you will
remain subject to death.

The Gospel of Thomas

The purpose of things in your life
is not for you to love them, but
to love the Self in all things.

The Upanishads

When you understand yourselves
you will understand everything.
Then you will realize that you
are God's children.

The Gospel of Thomas

To recognize the One, mediate on the Self.
Then you will go beyond joy and sorrow.

The Upanishads

Understand the Self within and know that
you are already living God's Kingdom.

The Gospel of Thomas

Recognize that all things exist in the
One, and you will become the One.

The Bhagavad Gita

One will not find himself by seeking
among transient things.

The Buddha

While the wise man may dress in rags,
his heart holds the greatest of riches.

The Tao Te Ching

All things are transient and subject to
decay. To become attached to things leads
to suffering. One can not truly say this
belongs to me, or this is what I truly am.
The answer to all things cannot be found in
the outer world of things or self-concepts.

The Buddha

He who identifies himself with the world,
receives the world. He who sees himself
as the world comes to accept it.

The Tao Te Ching

One achieves self-realization by practicing
mental concentration. He will thus
come to the state of Noble Wisdom.

The Lankavatara Sutra

He who seeks knowledge accumulates
it each day. He who seeks wisdom
forgets all that he learns.

The Tao Te Ching

The I Am:
In the Presence of the Avatar

OM (AUM) is not an immaterial abstraction
which transcends the world of matter and earthly
existence; it is the world we live in but do not see.
It is here—now, I-Thou, and "the reality that flows."

—William Braden

One of the truly amazing parallels between Christian and Hindu texts is the use of the phrase "I Am." The author of the canonical Gospel of John has Jesus use these words quite often when referring to himself as the incarnation of God. Orthodox Christians took such phrases as "I and the Father are one" literally. Rather than understanding the statement in a mystical sense, they believed that Jesus, and no one else, could identify with God the Father.

Gnostic Christians, however, used the phrase "I Am" in its original, mystical, context. The Jesus who speaks these words in the Gnostic Gospels is not the historical teacher from Galilee; he is the eternal Christ, the avatar—the incarnation—of the Godhead who takes on human form again and again throughout human history. The Hindu avatar, Krishna, uses the phrase in precisely the same way. In fact, as the reader will discover, the "I Am" statements in both the *Bhagavad Gita* and the Gnostic Gospels are so similar in language and content that they are essentially interchangeable. In these texts, Krishna and Christ are transparent beings who channel the voice of God.

The use of the term, "I Am," is also familiar to every Jew. In the Hebrew Bible, these words are the "name" of God: "Yahweh," which is variously translated as "I Am," "I Am that I Am," or "He who Is." The word, Yahweh, is related to the Hebrew verb "to be," but goes beyond that sense to suggest the active presence. It implies that God is immanent in our lives.

This "active presence" word for God, however, did not originate with the Jews. As a name for God, it was well known among all Semitic peoples long before the advent of monotheism. It is possible that ancestors of the Hebrews picked up the term during their sojourn as slaves in Egypt. The tribe of Levi, to which Moses belonged, knew the word and knew that it was often used in a shortened form— Yo! Yah! or Yahu!—as a mantra.

Both the ancient Egyptian priests and the Brahmins of India understood the fundamental principles of vibro-therapeutics. Both those religions used sacred syllables as chants and mantras to set up vibratory reactions that were useful for healing. Their toning was also used to stimulate latent centers of human consciousness.

For the ancient Brahmins, as well as for modern Hindus, the sacred syllable, AUM, represents the primal sound of creation. It is considered to be the "hum" of the universe. Is it possible that there is a linguistic connection between the sacred Hindu syllable, AUM, and the Semitic name for God? Even the English "I Am" sounds much like the Sanskrit "AUM." Whatever the case, linguistically, both avatars of God, Christ and Krishna, incorporate the essence of Being-ness in their use of the expression "I Am."

I Am the Light which is upon them all.
I Am the All. All things came from Me
and all things will return to Me. Split
the timber and there I Am. Lift a stone
and you will discover Me there.

The Gospel of Thomas

I Am the origin of all things. All things
came from Me. Whether moving or
unmoving, all things exist in Me.

The Bhagavad Gita

I Am all existence. I Am mother, father,
child. Whether moving or unmoving, that I
Am. All that exists, exists in Me.
I Am the womb of life. I Am the invisible
one who dwells in all things.

The Trimorphic Protennoia

I Am the Father of the Universe,
and I Am the source of the Father.
I Am the Mother of the Universe,
and the source of the Mother.
Beyond Me nothing exists.

The Bhagavad Gita

I exist in every soul. I awaken those who
sleep. My voice cries out in every creature.
I have existed from the beginning.

The Trimorphic Protennoia

I Am the self-existent One. I can be found
in every heart. I Am the beginning; I Am
the middle; and I Am the end of all things.

The Bhagavad Gita

I Am manifest in those who love Me.
Silence is my dwelling place, yet
those who seek Me will hear Me.

The Trimorphic Protennoia

I Am the Soul which dwells in all things;
I Am their beginning, middle and end.

The Bhagavad Gita

I Am the seed that is planted in every being.
I Am Father, Mother, and child.
I Am the incorruptible One,
and I dwell within you.

The Apocryphon of John

I Am the foundation that supports
the heavens, the Light that shines
everywhere; the joy of all souls.

The Manichean Psalms

I Am the bread of life; he who comes
to Me shall not hunger, and he who
believes in Me shall never thirst.

The Gospel According to John

I can be heard in all things. My speech
is beyond grasping. I alone exist.

The Thunder: Perfect Mind

I Am the Father and Mother of all
things. Without Me nothing can exist.
I am the Way; I am refuge; I am your
friend. I see and support all things.

The Bhagavad Gita

I Am the sweet fragrance of the
earth, the life in all beings.

The Bhagavad Gita

For those who focus on Me
with a singleness of purpose,
I Am easily attainable.

The Bhagavad Gita

I Am the eternal seed of all beings,
the intellect of all intelligence, and
the heroism of all heroics.

The Bhagavad Gita

I Am you and you are Me. Where you
are, there also Am I. I Am planted
in all things, and when the harvest
comes, it is I which you reap.

The Gospel of Eve

My love is equal for all beings. I can
be reached through devotion, for
I Am in them, and they in Me.

The Bhagavad Gita

I Am the life of the world. I Am
sweet water and the sap in trees.

The Manichean Psalms

I Am the wetness in water, the light of
the sun, and the radiance of the moon.

The Bhagavad Gita

I Am she in whom all things come to be.
I Am movement of all that moves.
I Am Mind that dwells in the Light.
I Am invisible and manifest in all things.
I Am beyond measure and there are
no words which can describe Me.

The Trimorphic Protennoia

I Am time beyond time. I sustain all
things. I Am life and I Am death. I Am the
knowledge of those who know Me. Among
the hidden mysteries, I Am the silent One.

The Bhagavad Gita

I Am that which came into being at the
beginning. I Am the Beloved,
and the one who alone is righteous.
I speak so that you may hear Me.
Focus on Me so that you may see Me.

The [Second] Apocalypse of James

I Am the unborn, everlasting Lord of All.
I Am born into the realm of nature.
I Am AUM, the eternal Word. I Am
the prayer that is made in silence.

The Bhagavad Gita

I Am a mirror; see yourself in Me. I Am
a door, so knock upon Me. I Am your
resting place, so rest yourself within Me.

The Hymn of Jesus from *The Acts of John*

I pervade all things, both manifest
and un-manifest. All things and
all beings exist in Me.

The Bhagavad Gita

I Am a lamp,
so that you might see Me.
I Am a path for you to travel.

The Hymn of Jesus from *The Acts of John*

I exist in the hearts of all those
who worship Me. I Am the light of
wisdom that dispels the darkness.

The Bhagavad Gita

I Am the Holy Father, the Living One
who reveals all things that are hidden.
If you understand Me,
you will become what I Am.
Reach out and take hold of Me.

The [Second] *Apocalypse of James*

I Am the Father, the Mother, the
Sustainer, the Grandfather, the Purifier,
the One thing to be known.

The Bhagavad Gita

I Am the perfect Thought of the Invisible One. Through Me, all things came into being.

The Trimorphic Protennoia

I Am knowledge contained within the soul. I Am time that never ends. I Am the Creator who sees His creation. I Am death, the end of all things; and I Am the source of all that will yet come to be.

The Bhagavad Gita

I Am the beginning and the end. I Am the One who is honored and the One who is rejected. I Am that which is holy, and the One who is defiled. I Am the virgin and I Am the Mother. I Am the One who is barren, and I have many children.

The Thunder: Perfect Mind

I Am the beginning and the end. I Am the sacrifice and the offering. I Am the sacred gift, sacred food, sacred words, and the holy fire into which all offerings are made.

The Bhagavad Gita

I Am in that place which knows no division.

The Gospel of Thomas

I pervade the Universe. Know that I Am.

The Bhagavad Gita

Cutting the Ties That Bind:
The Path of Renunciation

Do not be afraid. I am rich.
I will fill you with my wealth.

—The Gospel of the Savior

One of my spiritual heroes is Mahatma Gandhi. History records his heroic exploits in freeing India from British rule and vastly improving the lot of the Indian people. Many people are familiar with Gandhi's lasting model for non-violent civil disobedience. Like Jesus, the Mahatma was a living example of ahimsa, or non-violence, in the face of oppression. And, like Jesus, Gandhi not only turned his own cheek, but taught his people the value of overcoming violence and hate with peace and love.

For Gandhi, the search for truth required that he follow the path of renunciation—being in the world, without being of it. The practical application of renunciation was, for Gandhi, and all others who have ever taken such vows, to strip away virtually everything in life that stands between oneself and God. While much of Gandhi's autobiography is devoted to the actions and events of his life on the world stage, it also chronicles his journey of self-conquest through gradual transformation.

The Mahatma was born Mohandas K. Gandhi in Porbandar, India, in 1869. His family was one of privilege, and his young life was one of ease and comfort. At the tender age of thirteen, Gandhi married his life-long wife, Kasturbai. As a young adult he took up the practice of law, and looked forward to a life as a typical and successful member of the middle class, with all the materialism such a life implies.

Then Gandhi's life began to change. By the time he was assassinated many years later, the Mahatma owned only seven possessions: his spectacles, his begging bowl, his loincloth, his sandals, and one copy each of the *Bible*, the *Bhagavad Gita*, and the *Koran*.

Sitting at the feet of my own guru from India (Eknath Easwaran) during the 1960s, I loved to hear him tell stories about the Mahatma (Great Soul), whom he had met as a child. One such story had to do with Gandhi's attendance at summit meetings with other world leaders: Joseph Stalin, Franklin D. Roosevelt, and Winston Churchill. Gandhi was deeply bothered by both the smoke and smell of cigars, so whenever he attended a summit he would intentionally seat himself next to Winston Churchill, just so he could light his cigars for him. By these physical acts, Gandhi conquered his aversion to smoke, and practiced compassion at the same time.

Another favorite story is about a mother who came to Gandhi one day with her young son in tow. "Gandhiji," she pleaded, "please tell my son to stop eating sugar." Gandhi told her, "Come back in three days." Puzzled, the mother did as she was asked and went back home. When she returned with her son three days later, Gandhi told the boy, "Stop eating sugar." The mother then asked Gandhi, "Why didn't you just tell him to stop eating sugar three days ago?" "Because," the Mahatma said, "three days ago I hadn't stopped eating sugar myself."

Inevitably, the day arrived in his married life when Gandhi decided it was time to let go of sex and take a vow of celibacy. His long-suffering wife was not at all pleased by this decision, but she understood her husband's purpose in taking this vow. Difficult as it was for her, Kasturbai always supported her husband's feats of spiritual athleticism in the end.

What Gandhi practiced in life, he practiced in the act of dying as well. Eknath Easwaran, in his book, *Gandhi the Man*, describes the last moments of the last day in Gandhiji's life:

Gandhi was in Delhi, consuming every waking moment in a last plea for Hindu–Muslim unity. When it came time for the prayer meeting he walked to it briskly, as he always did, with his arms on the shoulders of two of the ashram girls. A dense crowd had gathered to hear him speak. As he walked to the platform through the crowd, Gandhi held his palms together in front of him in greeting. As he did so, a young man blinded with hatred placed himself in Gandhi's path, greeted him with the same gesture of his hands, and fired a gun point-blank into Gandhi's heart. Such is the greatness of this little man's love that as his body fell, nothing but the mantram that was deep within him came to his lips, *Rama, Rama, Rama*. It meant *I forgive you, I love you, I bless you.*[13]

Saint Francis of Assisi renounced the world in a slightly different way. The story goes that Francis, being born into a wealthy family like the historical Buddha, one day had a mystical experience of God that immediately changed his life and the way he looked at material possessions and social status. Unlike Gandhi, who let worldly things drop away one at a time, Saint Francis was said to have taken all of his possessions, including the clothes he was wearing, and thrown them out the window of his father's house, into the eager arms of those less fortunate. Then Francis, quite naked, walked out the front door and never looked back. From that moment on, Francis devoted every moment of his life to the service of God through his service to the sick, the poor, and the outcast.

The path of renunciation has never been a popular path for the vast majority of the human race, and it is especially unpopular for those of us who live in a culture that worships power, possessions, and pleasure above all else. For Christians—outside of Catholic monastic traditions—Jesus' clear call to leave the world in favor of the Kingdom of God has been pretty much ignored.

Nevertheless, Jesus, Krishna, the Buddha, and Lao Tzu all considered renunciation a necessary part of the spiritual path that cannot be avoided if one wishes to achieve enlightenment in this lifetime. But the path of the renunciate is a path that only a few will ever take in any age. Such a journey is even harder to contemplate for those of us who live in a materialistic culture that places little value on spiritual pursuits.

Neither do we have any cultural models. There may be Catholic monasteries and nunneries where voluntary poverty and celibacy is practiced, but even these few mod-

---

13 Eknath Easwaran, *Gandhi the Man: How One Man Changed Himself to Change the World,* Tomales, CA, Nilgiri Press, 2011, p. 166.

els are safely hidden away. We don't have the benefit of living in a spiritually oriented culture where temples, wandering sadhus, monks, and nuns with shaved heads and begging bowls are integral parts of the social fabric. In our culture, poverty is usually seen as failure, and celibacy is only practiced by pre-teens.

But every once in a while we might catch a glimpse of what it really means to devote one's entire life to God, and to nothing else. For me, the clearest memories of what it means to become a renunciate come from the 1960s and '70s when I was young, didn't own much anyway, and had taken up the hippie lifestyle—which had a natural disdain for all things material.

After graduating from seminary in 1970, I was ordained by the American Lutheran Church, and became the national Church's one and only pastor to the "Counter Culture." I didn't exactly look like a Lutheran pastor—not with my long hair, beads, bells, bell-bottoms and bare feet—so the Church really didn't know what to make of me. The bishop, the pastors, and the laity supposed I looked the way I did so that I could better minister to young people. And I didn't try to convince them otherwise.

The focus of my ministry was a halfway house I opened to take in young people with a variety of problems: teenagers, as well as young men and women who needed counseling and emotional support as much as they needed food and shelter.

The national office of the Church funded the ministry to the extent that it paid for the facility and my meager salary. With no allocation for food, I had to raise money outside of the Church, but I was never able to generate enough money to pay for the staff I badly needed. However, I could offer volunteers room and board in exchange for time and talent. For young people back then, food and shelter was often more than enough. Voluntary poverty for the Counter Culture was actually a source of pride—being both a spiritual lifestyle, and a political statement.

Our very first volunteer was a young man who did the cooking for the household. David was twenty-two years old, and was a very gentle soul. His warmth seemed to be generated by the energy of light alone, and he was not materialistic in any way.

All of us loved David, which is why we were all very happy for him when, after a number of months with us, he met the girl of his dreams and asked her to marry him. Even though this meant he would be leaving us to live with his new bride, we wished David all the happiness in the world.

David was also a very handsome young man, and his fiancé was both a wonderful person and quite beautiful. The pair were a storybook couple, and we thought of them as a fairy tale prince and princess who would live happily ever after.

Finally the wedding day rolled around, and I performed the simple ceremony. We all kissed the bride, congratulated the groom, and threw rice as David and his princess got into their carriage and headed off on their honeymoon.

The trouble with fairy tales is that they don't always have happy endings. As the newly married couple were driving down the Big Sur coast—with its narrow two lanes and hairpin curves, high above the roiling sea—something happened that caused David's car to veer off the road. It crashed through the barriers at the edge of the perilous cliffs and became airborne. We never learned what caused the accident, or exactly what had happened. All we knew for sure was that David and his beautiful bride plunged a thousand feet to their deaths—on the happiest day of their lives.

We were still grieving for these young people the day Steven came to us. Like David, he had no possessions other than the clothes on his back. And no shoes. Stephen had stopped wearing shoes years before, he told us, because—if you wear shoes, the whole earth is covered with leather (or rubber or whatever.) The point being that you can't truly feel the earth unless you walk upon it with bare feet.

Steven, like David, was an especially gentle soul, and all of us quickly came to see him as a sadhu, a wandering holy man. Steven's words were soft and kind, but the major influence he had on the household was due to the example he set. Steve was a vegetarian, so the house became vegetarian. Steven wore no shoes, so we took ours off as well. Now we could actually feel Mother Earth supporting us.

Once a week my wife would go to the supermarket with fifty dollars—all that we could afford to feed a dozen people for a week—and a general shopping list from Steven. From this, Steven provided three meals a day, seven days a week, using just what we had available, and none of us ever went hungry.

As a spiritual discipline, Steven fasted one day a week, so several of us started fasting one day a week as well. Twice a year—the week before Christmas and the week before Easter, Steven would fast for seven straight days. He prepared a feast on Christmas day, and again on Easter Sunday. He served dinner and sat down with us, sharing grace and our company. And while the rest of us stuffed ourselves like turkeys, Steven maintained his fast.

Although Steven never bought anything for himself, he encouraged me to buy—for the house—all seven albums by the Moody Blues. He then turned us on to the profound spiritual message in these recordings, and we probably listened to every album—Steven's Bible—a thousand times.

One day, after several years had passed, Steven announced that it was time for him to move on. He said his goodbyes, and we all had tears in our eyes as we hugged him. Then the young sadhu turned and walked out of our lives forever. He left with just the clothes on his back . . . and no shoes.

Steven was a rare example of what it means to be a spiritual "athlete." He was a hero in that he had succeeded in conquering himself. Most of us, at least in this lifetime, won't become renunciates. But we can gain inspiration and strength from hearing the stories, and reading the words, of those who have.

There was a wealthy man who said to himself, "I should fill my storehouses with grain, and then I will be secure." This was his intention, but that very night he died.

The Gospel of Thomas; parallels: Matthew, Luke

People think that all they gain in life is really theirs. They boast of their wealth, and revel in it. But by being addicted to the gratification of their senses, they will create hell for themselves.

The Bhagavad Gita

Jesus sent out his disciples saying, "Take no gold, nor silver, nor copper in your belts. Take no bag, no staff, no sandals, nor a second tunic—for the laborer is worth his food."

The Gospel According to Mark; parallels: Matthew, Luke

With a heart unattached to the outer world, those who seek Me find joy and happiness.

The Bhagavad Gita

Do not store up for yourselves earthly possessions, which moths and rust can destroy, and robbers can steal. Rather, store up heavenly treasures which cannot be destroyed or stolen. For wherever your heart is, there is your treasure as well.

The Gospel According to Matthew; parallels: Luke, Thomas

The desire for wealth can not bring happiness. Instead, anxiety results from the desire to keep it. Wealth creates dissatisfaction, and the loss of it is like death. Those who seek wealth only increase their desires.

Santiparva Mahabharata

It is easier for a camel to pass through the eye of a needle than for a rich man to enter the Kingdom of God.

The Gospel According to Mark; parallels: Matthew, Luke

Those whose happiness is within, whose peace is within, whose light is within—that person becomes free.

The Chandogya Upanishad

People believe that their property and family belong to them. But nothing belongs to us. So this false belief can only lead to suffering.

The Dhammapada

A bird, wherever it goes, is happy because it is free of burdens. The monk who travels is happy with a single set of robes and a bowl for his daily food. He goes here and there, taking with him only the bare necessities.

The Khuddaka Patha Sutra

One buries treasure in the belief that it will be needed in the future. It is far better to act with charity and goodness. One who controls himself builds up hidden treasure that no thief can steal.

The Khuddaka Partha Sutra

There are two paths: one is directed towards wealth, the other towards freedom. The monk who understands this renounces worldly desires.

The Dhammapada

Fame, power, wealth, and pride—such things bring about their own doom.

The Tao Te Ching

The wise man moves about, not caring about home or possessions. He lives simply. His feet leave no footprints. Thus, the perfect person is one whose vessel is empty.

Chuang Tzu

A wealthy man can never be at peace even if he owns mansions full of gold and jewels. Then he has to guard his wealth against theft. In the end, this will destroy him.

The Tao Te Ching

Those who are concerned with their lives make themselves miserable. Even when they have what they want, they aren't happy. They only want more.

Chuang Tzu

What does it profit a man if he gains the whole world and loses his own soul?

The Gospel of the Egyptians; parallels: Matthew, Mark, Luke, John

Insatiable desires only lead to ruined souls.

The Bhagavad Gita

Those who seek pleasurable things already have their treasure. But the pleasures of the world are an illusion. Gold and silver are without substance.

Dialogue of the Savior

Things of the world are transitory. If one dies without first having realized the Self, there is no happiness here, or hereafter.

The Chandogya Upanishad

Go and sell what you have, and give the money to the poor. Then you will have riches in heaven.

The Gospel According to Mark; parallels: Matthew, Luke

Eternity can not be realized by those who are deceived with the illusion of worldly things.

The Upanishads

Those who love life will lose it. Those who hate life in this world will preserve it in eternity.

The Gospel According to John

One who has renounced the world reaches the highest pinnacle.

The Santiparva Mahabharata

One who renounces the world
does no harm to others.

The Majjhima-Nikaya

The person who lets the world control
him no longer possesses his inner self.

Chuang Tzu

Right resolve is to renounce
money and gold.

The Kevaddha Sutra

That person is wise who leaves gold
buried in the mountain, and
pearls beneath the sea.

The Tao Te Ching

Re-birth is a certainty for those
who crave sensory pleasures.

The Majjhima-Nikaya

True riches come from giving out of
one's abundance to those in need.

The Tao Te Ching

If you wish to be free from old age and
rebirth, become an island unto yourself,
and eliminate all your imperfections.

The Dhammapada

As fresh as morning breeze, feeling
reborn, I wander here and there
without a care in the world. Let others
chase after wealth. I am content with
the gifts provided by Mother Tao.

The Tao Te Ching

The disciples of John marry, but my disciples remain chaste like angels in heaven.

The Book of John the Evangelist

One who has recognized the Self within, and who is free of lust and anger, achieves ultimate freedom.

The Bhagavad Gita

A man who is married should not leave his wife, but someone who is not married should not marry.

The Gospel of the Egyptians

Those who seek God alone should leave home. The ancients understood this, and had no desire for families.

The Upanishads

Not everyone can accept these words, but only those who are ready. There are eunuchs by birth, and there are eunuchs who have been made eunuchs by men, and there are eunuchs who have made themselves eunuchs for the sake of the kingdom of heaven.

The Gospel According to Matthew

The highest achievement results from mastering one's senses. Wisdom comes when we are no longer interested in worldly things.

The Santiparva Mahabharata

Lust keeps humanity in bondage as long as people seek after those things that change and pass away.

The Book of Thomas the Contender

The wise man ceases seeking worldly pleasures. Thus, he reaches the highest goal.

The Santiparva Mahabharata

Only by renouncing passions of the flesh can one be truly free. This is not possible for the householder.

The Tevigga Sutra

Where passions are established, heavenly things cannot be realized.

Chuang Tzu

As long as there is even the slightest desire on the part of a man for a woman, the mind is still imprisoned.

The Dhammapada

A wise man does not desire or value things of this world.

The Tao Te Ching

One rises to the greatest virtue when he becomes celibate.

The Kevaddha Sutra

Physical hunger must be satisfied, but the wise man pays no attention to what his eyes see.

The Tao Te Ching

To escape bondage one should renounce the world—no matter how difficult this is.

The Itivuttaka Sutra

If our inner eye were to suddenly open, lust and greed would cease to exist.

The Tao Te Ching

Wisdom and Knowledge

The foolish reject what they see, not what they think;
the wise reject what they think, not what they see . . .
Observe things as they are and
don't pay attention to other people.

—Huang-Po

M ost of us aren't born with wisdom, although wisdom is latent within us. Knowing this—wishing to become wise—we may go looking for wisdom, but find that it eludes us time and again. We may read hundreds, even thousands, of books—all of the world's sacred scriptures, all of the teachings of all the spiritual masters who have ever lived—and still, wisdom may escape us.

True wisdom may be gained through living life, and learning from it. But wisdom is ultimately a product of the intuitive mind, not the thinking mind. Gnostic Christians called the opening of the intuitive mind "gnosis," or knowledge. Gnosis is not intellectual knowledge, but a deep understanding of how Reality works.

Gnosis, Knowledge, Wisdom—whatever we may choose to call the knowing Self within us—is what happens to us after we exhaust the intellectual mind. Life's "aha!" experiences are flashes of insight that come to us in an instant, without effort. Gnosis happens when our thinking minds are looking the other way. Zen Buddhists refer to such sudden insight as "satori," and Christians might call it "revelation."

Gnostic Christians spoke of gnosis as "secret" knowledge, yet it is secret only to the extent that most of us don't have spiritual "eyes that see." We miss the deep meaning of life due to our craving for material existence. And if we ever transcend our limited perception, gnosis will come in a flash of insight, not from a well thought out paper on philosophy.

If we are unable to see the Kingdom of God, both within us, and all around us, it is only because our perception is focused on the kingdom of Earth. When Jesus was questioned as to whether or not he considered himself a king, he replied that his kingdom was "not of this world."

Many *New Testament* scholars today like to think of Jesus as a wisdom teacher in the tradition of the Greeks. But Jesus taught the wisdom of God, not of men. In his book, *Meeting Jesus Again for the First Time*, Marcus Borg, a *New Testament* scholar and professor of religion at Oregon State University, calls Jesus' wisdom, like Lao Tzu's and the Buddha's, "world subverting wisdom." Such deep insight flies in the face of conventional wisdom and encourages people to look at life in entirely new ways. It suggests that happiness may be more important than pleasure, and serenity more important than achieving, acquiring, and "being right." Like a Zen master, Jesus used parables and aphorisms to shock people out of their conventional thinking.

The wisdom tradition of Jesus was even more pronounced in Gnostic Christianity. The word for "wisdom" in the Hebrew Bible, and in Gnostic Christian texts, is feminine in nature, and when translated into Greek becomes "Sophia." Gnostic Christians allegorized Sophia as the divine Mother, and in some texts Sophia was featured as the spiritual consort of the Christ.

Most of us recognize that intellectual knowledge is not the same thing as wisdom, and yet (and I am the greatest of all offenders) we often act as if our intellectual mind will eventually produce profound spiritual awareness. Jesus, the Buddha, Krishna, and Lao Tzu tell us that it cannot. The intellect, for all of its merits, is not in charge of perception.

Wisdom and knowledge find
those with a pure heart.

Dialogue of the Savior

I abide in hearts out of compassion,
replacing ignorance and darkness
with a shining lamp.

The Bhagavad Gita

Be wise like the fisherman who caught
many fish. He kept the biggest fish,
and returned the rest to the sea.

The Gospel of Thomas

The wise, meditating on the Self, recognize
God who is hidden within the darkness.
Joy and sorrow are left far behind.

The Upanishads

The wise person who seeks truth is
fortunate. Once he has found it, he is at
peace, and nothing can disturb him.

The Book of Thomas the Contender

Mastering the senses, one achieves wisdom.
Attaining wisdom, one finds inner peace.

The Bhagavad Gita

Understand what is here and now and
you will understand all mysteries.

The Gospel of Thomas

When ignorance is overcome through
knowledge of the Self, God is revealed.

The Bhagavad Gita

Choosing the path of wisdom, become aware of those things which lead you forward, and those which hold you back.

The Buddha

Perfect wisdom comes spontaneously to those who seek it.

Chuang Tzu

Studying many scriptures is pointless if one does not practice the wisdom contained within them.

The Dhammapada

The fisherman forgets the fish trap once he has caught the fish. It is the same with words. Once the idea is grasped, words become useless.

Chuang Tzu

Wisdom is achieved by those who overcome their natural resistance to diligent practice.

The Dhammapada

If one is seeking wisdom, there is no need to leave home.

The Tao Te Ching

Wise is that person who sees reality behind the illusion.

The Buddha

With the sight and hearing of a child, the wise person makes no distinction between this and that. He simply sees what is in front of him.

The Tao Te Ching

Wisdom is the seeking of truth, and anyone who seeks the truth will avoid the traps in life that destroys the spirit.

The Book of Thomas the Contender

Understanding immortality, those who are wise do not seek for truth among those things which are impermanent.

The Upanishads

Do not give to dogs what is holy, and do not cast your pearls before pigs, lest they trample them underfoot, and then turn and tear you apart.

The Gospel According to Matthew; parallel: *Thomas*

Those who are wise should not disturb the peace of those who are ignorant.

The Bhagavad Gita

Seek wisdom earnestly through learning. Practice wisdom by being faithful, loving, and charitable.

The Apocryphon of James

Once you have understood the Self, seek the wisdom of yoga [union with the divine], In this way you will free yourself from karma [action].

The Bhagavad Gita

Wise people and fools cannot live together because it is like mixing oil with water.

The Book of Thomas the Contender

Once knowledge is comprehended, those who are wise find peace. Those who lack knowledge will find no joy in this life or the next.

The Bhagavad Gita

The body is a fragile thing. It must
be protected against evil by the
strong walls of wisdom.

The Dhammapada

If fool comes into the presence of
wisdom, he still can't comprehend it.

The Buddha

Those who are wise mold their lives
in the same way carpenters shape
wood, farmers water crops, and
archers aim their arrows.

The Buddha

Wisdom comes by cultivating the mind.
Cultivating the mind comes by associating
with positive people, following the
dharma, and maintaining right attitude.

The Buddha

Wisdom is knowing others;
enlightenment is knowing oneself.

The Tao Te Ching

A wise man teaches others
without using words.

Chuang Tzu

A wise person finds value in things
others throw away, and gets rid of
things others find valuable. In this way,
he becomes fit to guide others.

The Tao Te Ching

Those who are wise have an inner light,
so they succeed in helping others.

The Tao Te Ching

Everyone who understands what I am saying can be compared to a wise man who built his house on rock. The rains fell, the floods came, and the winds blew and beat against his house, but it did not fall because its foundation was rock.

The Gospel According to Matthew; parallel: Luke

Defend yourselves against the world. Erect fortifications to protect yourselves so that the world does not rob you of your birthright. If you do not do this, then those things that you fear the most will come to pass.

The Gospel of Thomas

Who, then, is the faithful and wise servant, whom his master has set over his household to give them their food at the proper time? Blessed is that servant who remains faithful, for the master will set him over all his possessions.

The Gospel According to Matthew; parallel: Luke

Wisdom has been achieved by the yogi who has gained control over his sense organs and sees everything in the world as equal, whether it be rocks or gold.

The Bhagavad Gita

Among those with virtue there are four types of people who seek Me: those who experience sorrow, those who seek knowledge, those who seek pleasure, and those who have attained wisdom. Among these four types of people, it is the wise person devoted to Me who surpasses all others. I am dear to him, and he is dear to Me.

The Bhagavad Gita

At the end of many births, the wise person takes refuge in Me—realizing that all things are the Self. Rare and wonderful is the soul that achieves this state of consciousness.

The Bhagavad Gita

The wise are no longer influenced by the vagaries of life or the opinions of others. They are like rocks which cannot be blown away by the wind.

The Dhammapada

Those who are unaware of the true nature of life, and who do not follow the dharma, are those without wisdom. Wise are those who achieve balance in life. They become serene and are immune to good and evil.

The Dhammapada

Those young in the dharma may lose their vigilance, but those who are wise will guard it carefully—for they treasure it above all things.

The Dhammapada

Earth and sky exist for aeons because they have no personal desires. Wisdom is found by people who live for others. The wise do not seek to be first, but to be last. Those who deny themselves find security in being selfless; thus, they are fulfilled.

The Tao Te Ching

Wise is the person who has no preferences for one thing over another. He allows his heart to become empty of desires.

The Tao Te Ching

Once you have achieved understanding, let that be enough. Do not show off. Give up pride. To go ahead is to go backward. This is not the Way, and all things that oppose the Way will soon cease to be.

The Tao Te Ching

Be as wise as serpents and
as innocent as doves.

The Gospel of Thomas; parallels: *Matthew, Luke*

The wise person keeps silent and
controls his mind. That which he
knows, he keeps to himself.

The Upanishads

Those who are wise take care of those who are virtuous and faithful.

The Maha-parinibbana Sutra

One who knows should remain silent.

The Tao Te Ching

Love and Compassion

All you need is love.

—The Beatles

One of the greatest embodiments of love and compassion in our time is the Dalai Lama. Exiled from his homeland many years ago when the Chinese communists invaded Tibet, the Dalai Lama has nevertheless become an ambassador of love to the entire world—ceaselessly traveling from one land to another, sharing goodwill. When asked what his religion is, he does not begin a long dissertation on the nature of Tibetan Buddhism. Instead, he says simply, "My religion is love." Even though the Chinese government hates and fears him, he refers to them as "my friends, the enemy."

How many of us, having endured what the Dalai Lama has, could respond to such hatred with such love? No doubt, most of us fail to live up to our own expectations when it comes to acting in a loving way. Jesus said that it is easy to love those who love us, and hard to love our enemies—and yet much of the time we find it difficult enough just to love those who love us.

I recall reading a story some years ago about an encounter that took place between a Jewish rabbi and his wife, and a member of a white supremacist group who hated Jews. Circumstances arose in which this young man, along with his brethren, broke into a local synagogue and destroyed much of it, defacing almost every surface with racial slurs and other slogans of intolerance.

If something like this were to happen to most of us, our first reaction might be one of equal anger and disgust. We would call the police with the hopes that the responsible parties would be found, arrested, and severely punished. We would probably feel horribly violated, and our intolerance of hate groups would become intense. Some of us might even want to retaliate in kind.

But instead of calling the police, the rabbi and his wife went looking for the responsible people. They were finally able to locate one member of the hate group, and instead of responding to him angrily, they told him that they loved him. This response so disarmed the man that, when the rabbi invited him to dinner at the couple's home, the man actually accepted the invitation.

After dinner, the rabbi and his wife talked with this young man for many hours, during which time he shared his life story with them. It was not surprising for the couple to learn that this poor lost soul had been abused and unloved as a child. Neither was it surprising to them that his role models had been parents who were bigots.

It was apparent to the rabbi and his wife that the young man's hatred had nothing to do with them, any more than it had to do with the fact that they were Jewish. They understood that this young person's hate was really an expression of his own pain and suffering. Life had been hard and cruel to him, so he had become hard and cruel to survive.

The rabbi and his wife did not see a hate-filled criminal before them—someone who ought to be vilified and punished. They saw a human being who was desperately in need of love and compassion. As it turned out, love worked a miracle: not only did the ex–white supremacist voluntarily repair all the damage his group had done to the synagogue, but he became like a son to the rabbi and his wife, and they became the loving parents he never had.

An inspiring true-life story like this allows us to see that love and compassion are more than spiritual platitudes. Hate really can be transformed by love, just as the great spiritual teachers have always told us. To see what we need to do in this world, to recognize the pain and suffering in everyone, we have to transform ourselves into living embodiments of love. If we succeed—through great effort, and many failures—we come to realize that what we did for the sake of others was the very thing we needed to do for ourselves. Love, like hate, returns to the sender.

Love your neighbor as yourself.

The Gospel According to Mark; parallels:
Matthew, Luke, Thomas

Recognizing what brings pleasure and pain to oneself, the true yogi treats others accordingly. Thus, he desires happiness for everyone, sorrow for no one.

The Bhagavad Gita

You have heard it said, "You should love your neighbor and hate your enemy." But I say to you, love your enemies and pray for those who persecute you, so that you might be children of your Father who is in heaven.

The Gospel According to Mark; parallels: Matthew, Luke

The true yogi, with his heart centered in Me, recognizes the Self in all beings, and acts accordingly.

The Bhagavad Gita

I was hungry and you fed me. I was thirsty and you gave me drink. I was a stranger and you welcomed me. I was naked and you clothed me, I was sick and you visited me. I was in prison and you came to me. What you did to the least of these, my brethren, you did also to me.

The Gospel According to Matthew

Whatever you do, whatever you eat, whatever you offer in sacrifice, whatever you give away, whatever renunciation you practice, know that you do these things as an offering to Me.

The Bhagavad Gita

Blessed are the merciful, for they will receive mercy.

The Gospel According to Matthew; parallel: Luke

Practice gentleness, seek truth, give up anger, do not slander, and have compassion for all beings. Be gentle, be modest, be useful to others. All these things belong to the one who wishes to see Me.

The Bhagavad Gita

Seeing himself in others, one who is in a state of higher consciousness feels compassion for all beings, and holds only positive thoughts about them.

Doctrinal formulas

The one who has excelled does only good for others, and treats everyone the same. He has compassion for the whole world.

The Anguttara Nikyaya

If you do not care for each other, who will? When you take care of others, when you care for the sick, you are caring for me as well.

The Buddha

When you see yourself in others, it is impossible to hurt anyone else.

The Buddha

Nothing but good comes to him who loves others as he loves himself.

The Tao Te Ching

The wise man has no need of anything, so he is able to give his full attention to others. He feels compassion equally for those who are concerned about others, and those who are not.

The Tao Te Ching

The world is transformed by those who love all people, just as you love yourself.

The Tao Te Ching

Compassion and mercy bring victory. Heaven belongs to the merciful.

The Tao Te Ching

You receive no benefit from loving only those who love you. Great benefit comes from loving those who hate you.

The Gospel of the Egyptians

Do not give food only to worthy people, but give it also to strangers. Turn no one away from your house. For what you give is what will be returned to you.

The Taittiriya Upanishad

Be compassionate, as your father in heaven is compassionate.

The Gospel According to Mark; parallels: *Matthew, Luke*

Seeing Me in all living creatures, know that love for all others is love for Me.

The Bhagavad Gita

You should never celebrate the downfall of those who are ignorant.

Agrapha

When evil men worship Me they should be regarded as good because they have found the right resolve.

The Bhagavad Gita

Your Father makes his sun rise on the good and the evil alike.

The Gospel According to Matthew and *Luke*

To Me, all beings are the same. I hate none, and no one is more dear to Me than another.

The Bhagavad Gita

Hate does not overcome hate. Only love overcomes hate. Knowing that we are all destined to die, why fight amongst yourselves?

The Buddha

In war, have mercy. True warriors do not carry arms. True fighters do not get angry. Those who wish to win should not be contentious. This is being in harmony with what is natural and pure.

The Tao Te Ching

The only way you can become free is to love those who hate you.

The Dhammapada

Do not turn away those you consider sinful and unworthy. If you have wisdom, you will try to save everyone.

The Tao Te Ching

Do not deceive anyone.
Do not turn away from anyone.
Never wish anyone harm.

The Buddha

If fields did not have weeds,
what would farmers do?

Chuang Tzu

Have compassion for all of creation.
Nurture within yourself
compassion that is limitless.

The Karaniya Metta Sutra

Wise men always seek to save everyone.
That way, nobody goes to waste.

The Tao Te Ching

Be compassionate as your heavenly father is compassionate.

The Gospel According to Mark; parallels: Matthew, Luke

When someone wants to take your shirt, let him have your coat as well. If someone forces you to go a mile with him, go with him an extra mile.

The Gospel According to Matthew;
parallels: Luke, Thomas

Give to one who begs from you, and do not turn your back on those who wish to borrow from you. Do not let one hand know what the other is doing.

The Gospel According to Matthew; parallel: Luke

Judas asked Jesus, "How do we begin our journey on this path?" Jesus said, "By being kind and loving."

The Gospel of the Hebrews; parallels Thomas

Whoever, in devotion, offers Me a gift, whether it be a flower, a fruit or water, I accept it as coming from one who has a pure heart.

The Bhagavad Gita

Just as a mother keeps her child from harm,
and guards him with her life, so you should
treasure all living beings. With a grateful
heart, spread love throughout the world.

The Buddha

The greatest reward in this world
is to take care of others. The greatest
loss in this world is to receive
from others without gratitude.

The Buddha

One should act without thinking
when performing acts of charity.

The Dhammapada

Encourage goodwill in the world
by being charitable and kind.

Doctrinal formulas

Good works
leave no tracks behind.

The Tao Te Ching

That your actions might be perfect, let your love flow without measure.

The Manichean Psalms

Even if one is firmly attached to the Void, if he does not have compassion for others he will make no progress toward reaching the final goal.

Saraha

Jesus went about the cities and villages, preaching the good news of the Kingdom and healing diseases and every infirmity. When he saw the crowds, he had compassion for them, because they were harassed and helpless. They were sheep without a shepherd.

The Gospel According to Matthew

When you cultivate an attitude of friendliness, little by little your own ill-will will diminish. When you cultivate an attitude of compassion, little by little your own annoyance will diminish. When you spread joy, little by little your aversion will diminish. When you consider all others as equal, little by little your revulsion will diminish.

The Majjhima Niyaka Sutra

I give you a new commandment: Love one another as I have loved you.

The Gospel According to John

Out of the abundance of your heart, cultivate love and compassion for all beings.

The Buddha

LOVE AND COMPASSION

Hypocrisy

*Always look at your moccasin tracks first
before you speak of another's faults.*

—Sauk saying

The warnings against hypocrisy voiced by Jesus, Buddha, Krishna, and Lao Tzu are never directed at the general public. They are directed toward those of us who claim to be religious or spiritual. Their criticisms might sting, but we should be grateful for them. Without recognizing the things we need to work on, we cannot grow. Puffing ourselves up, being in denial about our shortcomings, not taking responsibility for those times when we injure others by our thoughtlessness—are all attitudes that are self-defeating. Perhaps more than anything else, hypocrisy keeps us bound in the chains of illusion. If we do not practice what we preach, we are not self-aware. And if we are not self-aware, we are not growing.

None of this is news. We all know what hypocrisy is, and some part of us always knows when we are being hypocritical. It is our need to always justify ourselves that keeps us from hearing with open ears and seeing with open eyes. But we never really grow unless our defenses are down. Even our own inner voice can't get through to us unless we allow ourselves to become vulnerable. So, in a way, this chapter is as much about self-awareness as it is about hypocrisy. We can't fix something unless we know it's broken.

There are many similarities between Jesus and the historical Buddha. Their ethical and moral teachings are very similar. They both had life-altering mystical experiences. Both men began movements of religious renewal—Jesus within Judaism, Siddhartha Gautama within Hinduism. But there was one major difference between these two men: Jesus was a social prophet and a social critic, Buddha was not.

If we've had a Christian upbringing, one of the many images of Jesus that might come to mind is of him giving the religious hypocrites of his day a tongue-lashing. Supposedly, the subjects who bore the brunt of Jesus' challenges were the Pharisees—religious legalists who proclaimed that they were strict followers of the Mosaic Law, the Torah. Jesus accused these legalists of following the letter of the Law, while ignoring its spirit. He criticized them for making a show of their piety, while failing to put their piety into action. Simply put, these legalists didn't practice what they preached. And Jesus pointed this out to them.

But while Jesus is well known for his statements against hypocrisy, the following verses make it clear that he was hardly alone in this. Buddha, Krishna, and Lao Tzu were in full agreement with the man from Galilee.

Be careful that your spiritual practice is not done in public, so that others know that you are spiritual. When you give to charity, do not announce it like hypocrites do. Praise is their reward. Practice charity in secret and your Father will reward you in secret.

The Gospel According to Matthew; parallel: *Luke*

Those who are conceited, self-important, full of pride, and drunk with wealth honor Me in name only. They sacrifice to Me in name only. They hate Me within their own bodies because they are pretentious, full of ego and malice, lust for power, and are disrespectful of others.

The Bhagavad Gita

Not everyone who says to me, "Lord, Lord" will be saved, but only those who do works of righteousness.

The Gospel According to Matthew;
parallels: *Luke, Egyptians*

If you practice yoga but are conceited, you do not know Me at all. You have failed to understand My teaching, and you will not succeed.

The Bhagavad Gita

Stay away from people who consider themselves to be learned. They walk around in fine clothes and like to be noticed so that they might be honored in public. They take seats of honor in synagogues, and at feasts. These hypocrites steal from widows even as they repeat long prayers. The judgment that comes upon them will be great.

The Gospel According to Mark; parallels: *Matthew, Luke*

Those who perform spiritual practices in public so that they will be noticed and praised with honor and respect are unbalanced. Their ostentation will come to nothing.

The Bhagavad Gita

Renounce hypocrisy, for it is produced by evil intent. Hypocrisy leads you far away from the truth.

The Apocryphon of James

All actions are polluted that come from conceit, insincerity, and desire. These things are the result of evil thoughts.

The Bhagavad Gita

A monk is not a true monk until he has purified his own mind. Although he may wear a saffron robe, if he is not honest and doesn't control himself, he is not worthy of his robes.

The Dhammapada

Those who have heard my word, lifetime after lifetime, but have not practiced it, lifetime after lifetime, will only continue to suffer.

The Lotus of the True Law

Monks who seek recognition in order to gain influence and admiration, and monks who overwhelm others by insisting on their own point of view, only increase pride and passion.

The Kevaddha Sutra

Those who plant evil seeds will only harvest bitter fruit. These people are their own worst enemies.

The Dhammapada

Be careful not to display yourself in public. There is no sincerity in this. Such self-conscious acts are not in harmony with Tao, and will ultimately ruin a person.

Chuang Tzu

As the meaning of Tao was lost among humanity, it was replaced with intelligence. Along with intelligence came hypocrisy.

The Tao Te Ching

Follow the Way; but boasting and seeking recognition is not of the Way. One who is arrogant has already failed. There is no reward for those who are conceited, and no one can become a true leader by puffing themselves up.

The Tao Te Ching

The moment one stops following Tao, one also loses integrity at the same time.

The Tao Te Ching

Woe to you, scholars and Pharisees.
You hypocrites! Not only do you
refuse to enter the Kingdom, but you
keep others from doing so as well.

The Gospel According to Matthew;
parallels: Luke, Thomas

Whatever you teach others with words,
be sure to carry out in actions.

Agrapha

Wretched are you, scholars and Pharisees—
you hypocrites. You wash the outside of the
cup, but are full of filth within yourselves.

The Gospel According to Matthew;
parallels: Luke, Thomas

How is it that you see a splinter in someone
else's eye, but do not notice the log in
your own eye? This is hypocrisy! First,
remove the log in your own eye so that
you can see clearly enough to remove
the splinter from your brother's eye.

The Gospel According to Matthew;
parallels: Luke, Thomas

Fools dwell in the darkness, and are wise
only in their own conceit. Their vain
understanding serves no one. Rather, it
leads them to destruction. These enemies
of truth are blind men led by blind men.

The Upanishads

It doesn't matter how many spiritual
books you read if you don't practice
what they teach, what benefit is there
in not acting on holy words?

The Dhammapada

Lack of faith
on the part of one person
leads to faithlessness
on the part of others.

The Tao Te Ching

Don't worry about what others do
or don't do. Rather, pay attention
to what you do or fail to do.

The Dhammapada

Those who follow their own profane
theories cannot be corrected because
of their pride and hypocrisy. They know
nothing, and they do not follow the Buddha.

The Lotus of the True Law

Concentrate on your own faults—
the things you have done, and
the things you have left undone.
Ignore the faults of others.

The Dhammapada

It is not what goes into the mouth
that makes you unclean—
it is what comes out of your mouth.

The Gospel According to Matthew; parallels: *Luke, Thomas*

There are those of you who call me Lord, but do
not do the will of my Father, and do not follow my
teachings. Get away from me! I do not know you.

The Gospel According to Matthew; parallels:
Luke, Egyptians, Nazarenes

Grapes can't be picked from vines full of
thorns, nor can figs be taken from trees
with thorns. Bad fruit comes from bad trees
and good fruit comes from good trees.

The Gospel of Thomas; parallels: *Matthew, Luke*

Two men went into the Temple. One was a Pharisee
and the other was a tax collector. The Pharisee
prayed, "I give thanks to you, oh Lord, that I am
not like other men—extortioners, adulterers, even
this tax collector. I fast twice a week and I give
tithes from all I receive." The tax collector lifted
up his eyes to heaven, beat his breast and said,
"God, be merciful to me a sinner." I tell you, this
man returned home justified rather than the other.

The Gospel According to Luke

HYPOCRISY

There are those who are ashamed of things they shouldn't be ashamed of, and those people who are not ashamed of those things they should be ashamed of. Such people are following the wrong path.

The Dhammapada

Even though a monk takes ahold of my robes and follows me all about, but who is filled with desires, and whose mind is full of malice toward others—this monk is far from me and I am far from him.

A Sermon to Monks

For your own protection, place yourselves in the company of wise men, and resist being in the company of fools.

The Mangala Sutra

The fool that knows he is a fool is more fortunate than a fool who believes he is wise. This person only makes trouble for himself and others, and he suffers accordingly.

The Dhammapada

Suffering

Pain is inevitable, suffering is optional.

—Modern Buddhist wisdom

Orthodox Christians believe that suffering has meaning, especially the suffering of Jesus. For them, suffering is part of life. It cannot be avoided, and we shouldn't try to avoid it. Instead, we should learn to endure suffering. Suffering teaches us. Suffering tests us. Suffering makes us stronger.

This response to the reality of suffering is well illustrated in the story of Job, in the Biblical book of *Job*. Job, we are told, was a good and decent man. He was moral and upright in every way. He also had great faith in God.

Job was also blessed with all the good things life has to offer: health, family, and wealth. People in Job's circle considered the presence of all these good things to be evidence that if we are just moral and upstanding, and if we have faith in God, God will reward us materially.

But one day, Job's fortunes began to turn. His flocks were slain. His children were killed. And then Job got very sick. He developed sores from head to toe, and was in such misery that he came to curse the day he was born. When Job's friends saw what had happened to him, they said, in effect, "You must have sinned greatly for such calamities to have come upon you." But Job professed his innocence, knowing that he had not sinned.

In misery or not, Job's wife got tired of his whining, and said to him, "Do you still hold fast to your integrity? Curse God, and die." But Job rejected his wife's advice. He maintained his faith in God in spite of all his suffering.

Now the reader knows from the very beginning of this story that everything that befell Job was God's test. Satan (who was not yet a fallen angel) went to God and said, "Sure, Job loves you because he has all the good things of life. But would he remain faithful if you took them all away?" God pondered this awhile, and finally gave Satan permission to put Job to the test.

Even though Job suffered greatly, by the end of the story he has passed every test, so God restored him to health. The moral of the story being that if one's faith in God is true, it does not falter even in the worst of times.

So Judeo-Christianity views suffering as a test of faith and character. The Buddha, however, viewed suffering in an entirely different way. He wasn't interested in the question of whether or not suffering has meaning. He was more interested in finding the cause of suffering, and a means of ending it.

The Buddha noted that suffering always arises due to the indulgence of some form of desire. If our house burns down, we are miserable because we desire a house that hasn't burned down. When we get sick, we suffer because we crave health.

For most of us, most of the time, it's hard to remember that pleasure and pain always go hand in hand. We forget that we cannot have one without the other. So we seek to maximize pleasure and do our best to avoid pain. But the great masters knew that life doesn't work that way. Everything in our universe comes to us in pairs of opposites, and the opposites are always changing from one to the other. Pain replaces pleasure, pleasure replaces pain, over and over again, endlessly. Nothing in the material universe ever remains the same for long. But when we finally understand this truth at the most profound level, we have a chance to change the rules of the game.

Buddha taught that there is a way out of suffering, and that way is to eliminate desire. If we can retrain the mind so that it no longer craves, so that it no longer prefers one thing over another—so that good and bad, pleasure and pain, hot and cold, love and hate are all the same to us, then suffering ceases of its own accord.

If you understood the nature of suffering, you would not have to suffer. You must first understand what causes suffering, and then you will have the ability to transcend it.

The Hymn of Jesus from *The Acts of John*

When you experience things like heat and cold, pleasure and pain, you only feel them because your senses are in contact with them. These things come and go. These things have the nature of impermanence, so watch them come and go with patience and an even mind.

The Bhagavad Gita

Blessed are those who are persecuted; they will find rest in the Light.

The [Greek] *Gospel of Thomas*; parallels: *Matthew, Luke*

A person who remains steady and unattached when pleasure and pain comes and goes will achieve the highest goal.

The Bhagavad Gita

Jesus speaking to his brother, James, after his crucifixion: "I am not the body that surrounds me; therefore I did not suffer. At no time did I feel pain. No one harmed me at all. It was necessary that my body be destroyed."

The [First] *Apocalypse of James*

When, through diligent practice, yoga reaches its highest goal, and the Self is seen as God, the yogi is no longer affected by pleasure and pain—for his senses are no longer in contact with them.

The Bhagavad Gita

To transcend suffering, one must practice
with sincerity. Only with practice will
one be able to ascend to the top of
the mountain—which is wisdom.

The Dhammapada

I suffer because of my ego and
my selfishness. If I became
unselfish, how could I suffer?

The Tao Te Ching

Suffering proceeds from change and decay,
and is accompanied by pain and suffering.
These things are not part of essential mind.

The Buddha

That which is essential within a person
cannot suffer. That exists forever.

The Tao Te Ching

When one no longer considers anything
in the world his own, when he no longer
grieves for what no longer exists, when
he is no longer influenced by ideas
. . . he reaches a place of peace.

The Purabheda Sutra

This is why you get sick and die; you follow those things that mislead you.

The Gospel of Mary [Magdalene]

Grief and sorrow result from holding the world dear.

The Doctrine of the Buddha

Do not fear suffering, for you are surrounded by a protective wall of Spirit. The world has existed for a very long time, and it will continue to exist for a very long time. Your sufferings represent no more than an instant in time.

The Apocryphon of James

If you fear suffering, just do no evil deeds, either in secret or for all to see.

The Dhammapada

When you leave behind your suffering and the shame of your flesh and attain enlightenment, then you will become One, and will be One for all eternity.

The Book of Thomas the Contender

There is a place without substance. It exists beyond the Great Beyond. I call it the end of suffering.

The Buddha

Learn from these teachings. Understand knowledge and live life. Then, no one but yourself can cause you to suffer.

The Apocryphon of James

Gain wisdom, conquer lethargy by practice, and then you will transcend suffering.

The Dhammapada

Karma and Reincarnation

The snowdrop is a snowdrop and not an oak,
and just that kind of snowdrop, because it is
the outcome of the karma of an
endless series of past existences.

—Rhys-Davids

Karma and reincarnation are topics that cannot be discussed separately since they are inextricably linked. Karma is what *causes* reincarnation, or rebirth. Put an end to karma and you put an end to rebirth.

Karma, literally, means "works" or "actions." Since most of our actions in life have either positive or negative effects on ourselves and others, we can speak of accruing both "good" and "bad" karma during each lifetime. In theory, if our good karma outweighs our bad karma, our next birth will find us in circumstances that are more conducive to spiritual growth. If the opposite is the case . . . well, we don't even want to think about that.

Karma, we are told, is never neutral. If one becomes enlightened in any given lifetime that person may continue to act, but it is said that no karma of any kind is accrued. Enlightenment frees us from the wages of karma at the same time that it frees us from "samsara"—the ever-turning wheel of birth, death, and rebirth.

So who's keeping score? Dualistic religions like Judaism, Christianity, and Islam believe the scorekeeper is a supernatural Being who keeps a journal of debits and credits for each person. Eastern philosophies, by contrast, believe that we ourselves are the scorekeepers. But even if there is no supernatural being to pass judgment on us, it doesn't mean we get a pass. The law of karma suggests that *we* alone are responsible for all of the things that happen to us in this life and the next. Our specific karma is predicated upon everything that we have ever thought, said, or done in this life and all those that came before.

Traditional Christians might be surprised to learn that Hindus and Buddhists believe in "heaven" and "hell." But for Hinduism and Buddhism, such positive and negative realms have no location in time and space and are the product of our own karma. Like all phenomena, heaven and hell are devoid of ultimate reality. Like the life we are experiencing right now, they are projections of our own dualistic and deluded minds.

At least we should be happy to learn that "punishment," the feedback loop of karma and self-judgment, is never eternal. If we reap the negative effects of our actions here, and hereafter, these conditions last only as long as we choose them to. We can begin to alter our karma the moment we decide to leave the world behind and give our full attention and effort to the process of ending our suffering and achieving enlightenment.

Unlike their orthodox brethren, many Gnostic Christian movements believed in karma and reincarnation, although there are not a great number of references in the recovered texts. Contrary to the opinion of some, there are no references to reincarnation in the canonical Gospels of the *New Testament*. Certainly the historical Jesus understood the law of karma (we reap what we sow), but we have no idea what he believed about the afterlife. Many *New Testament* scholars believe that all of Jesus' references to judgment, the coming apocalypse, heaven, and so on. in the canonical Gospels, were not his words, but those of the Christian evangelists who wrote those Gospels.

No doubt there are at least some modern Christians who believe in reincarnation, but don't dare talk about it in church. Certainly this was the case with the early Church. The most famous orthodox Christian who believed in karma and reincarnation was the brilliant third-century apologist and theologian, Origen. There is no record that Origen bore the wrath of his brother clerics during his own time, but the Church excommunicated and anathematized him three centuries later just to set the record straight.

Origen cannot have been the only orthodox Christian who believed in the twin doctrines of karma and reincarnation, since these beliefs were specifically repudiated by the Church—not during the third century when Origen lived, but several centuries later. In 553 C.E. the Second Council of Constantinople decreed: "Whosoever shall support the mythical doctrine of the preexistence of the soul and the consequent wonderful opinion of its return, let him be anathema."

While the decree could be considered retroactive, and while it anathematized Origen officially, this could not have been its main purpose. For an anathema against reincarnation to be issued formally suggests that the belief was widespread among Christians even as late as the sixth century.

Reincarnation has always been a difficult doctrine to grasp because there are so many different interpretations about just how it works. The Buddhist understanding of "rebirth," for instance, differs from the Hindu belief in reincarnation—at least philosophically. To confuse matters even more, every philosophical system within each of these religions explains the doctrine in a slightly different way—all of which can be confusing to the Westerner who didn't grow up in any of these traditions.

Certainly the Tibetan Buddhists have concentrated on this subject far beyond the scope of other sects or religions. *The Tibetan Book of the Dead* is a guide and road map of what happens between death and rebirth. It is also a good place to begin for those who wish to know more about this subject.

Be merciful that you may obtain mercy. Forgive, so that you may be forgiven. As you judge, so you will be judged. As you serve, so will service be done to you. And whatever you measure out, that is what will be returned to you.

The Gospel According to Matthew; parallel: Luke

Agree with your adversary quickly while you are on the way with him, lest he deliver you to the judge, and the judge deliver you to his officer, and you are cast into prison. I tell you, you will not be released from that prison until you have paid the last farthing.

The Gospel According to Matthew; parallel: Luke

The soul of someone evil will be punished according to its transgressions. The virgin of light will blind that soul and hand it over to one of her judges to have it cast into a body which is appropriate for its crimes.

The Pistis Sophia

Everyone creates their own fate. Even life in the womb is affected by the karma from a previous life.

The Garuda Purana

Those who remain ignorant of Me, from one lifetime to the next, are born into wombs of those who are also ignorant. Trapped in delusion, they fall ever lower into the realms of existence.

The Bhagavad Gita

Into the wombs of cruel beings I cast malevolent and heartless persons who do evil—the most degraded of all those who exist in these worlds.

The Bhagavad Gita

From a sound, an echo returns. A body
creates a shadow. So, too, will misery
come to him who does evil works.

Three Sermons

If an evil person criticizes someone
who is virtuous, it is like spitting at the
sky. The spit doesn't dirty the sky, but
returns to pollute the person who spits.

Three Sermons

Adversity and suffering is the end of
all those who do evil in this life.

The Lotus of the True Law

The sheep need not fear wolves after this lifetime, nor anyone who can kill the body in this lifetime. They should fear, instead, those who have the power to kill both body and soul, and cast both into the flames of hell.

The Gospel of the Egyptians; parallels: *Matthew, Luke*

Seek now the meaning of all things so that your suffering may end. Do not wait, believing that you will find knowledge after you have taken on a new body.

The Pistis Sophia

Fate causes the old soul to forget all the many regions it has traveled over time, and all the punishments it has endured along the way. This forgetfulness becomes the body that surrounds the soul. It pretends to *be* the soul, but it is a false spirit.

The Pistis Sophia

Judge not, that you may not be judged. For with whatever judgment you pronounce, you will be so judged.

The Gospel According to Matthew; parallel: *Luke*

There are two eternal paths in this universe. One is of light, the other of darkness. The first leads to freedom from the wheel of birth, death, and rebirth; the other leads back to this world once more.

The Bhagavad Gita

If one does not find God in this lifetime, he is doomed to rebirth.

The Katha Upanishad

Many are the births you and I have passed through. I know them all, but you have forgotten.

The Bhagavad Gita

One's actions in life determine who that person is, and what befalls him. Those who do evil, become evil. Those who do good, become good. What we do in life determines our fate in this life and the next.

The Brihadaranyaka Upanishad

Those who seek happiness
in this lifetime by robbing others
of their happiness will find nothing
but misery after they die.

The Buddha

Do no evil, for suffering comes to those who
cause suffering. But suffering cannot assail
those who do good. Become a fortress,
both on the outside and within yourself,
so that nothing can overcome you. Life
is short; there is not a moment to lose.

The Dhammapada

Pleasures in life are like a flowing river. You float
away on them and are carried from lifetime
to lifetime. They pursue you like a hunter
pursues his prey. The cycle of birth, death, and
rebirth goes on and on. It is a long journey
for those who do not know the dharma.

The Dhammapada

Harm returns to the person who does harm.
It is like throwing dust into the wind.

The Dhammapada

Death and Immortality

For what is it to die but to stand naked in the wind and
to melt into the sun? And what is it to cease breathing,
but to free the breath from its restless tides,
that it may rise and expand and seek God unencumbered?

—Kahlil Gibran, *The Prophet*

Of all animal species on Earth, only Homo sapiens know they will die. Knowing this, all human beings have to face the fear of dying. It seems almost unimaginable that "I" will cease to exist. It seems ludicrous that our *experience* of reality will end in utter annihilation. Certainly total extinction has to be the most frightening thing we can imagine.

The ancients sought a remedy for the fear of dying, and developed religions to deal with the fear. Most of the ancient religions suggested that we don't really die, but live on in one form or another after our physical body goes back to the earth from which it came. Even though they wished to give their followers hope, how did these first religionists *know* what happened after death? Did they commit suicide so they could come back to life and explain what death was like? Or did they simply tell people to believe and have faith that their doctrines about death and the afterlife were accurate?

The problem is that everyone talks about death (if they dare mention it at all) from *this* side of the grave. Do any of us speak from experience? One of my favorite stories illustrating this question is about a Zen monk who asked his Zen master, "Roshi, is there life after death?" The Roshi answered, "I don't know." The monk was incredulous at this answer, and blurted out, "But Roshi, you're a Zen master." To which the Roshi replied, "Well yes, but I'm not a *dead* Zen master."

Tibetan Buddhists, on the other hand, claim to know a great deal about death and the process of dying—even the process of rebirth. *The Tibetan Book of the Dead* is purported to be a primer and navigational chart relating to what happens to us after death. It discusses what takes place as the body is dying, and the "bardo" planes of existence that we go through after we are dead. Tibetan Lamas even claim to remember their past incarnations—which can be confusing to the non-Buddhist because Buddhists do

not believe in a human soul. If there is no soul, what is it, then, that leaves the body at death? What is it that experiences the "lokas," or other worlds (or planes of existence) including heavenly and hellish realms, not to mention demons and deities? More puzzling still, what is it that is reborn? If "I" no longer exist, who or what takes on a new body? *What* has existed through countless incarnations? *What* can break the bonds of samsara and attain Nirvana?

Christians believe each one of us has a soul, but the belief that the soul flies off to heaven or hell immediately after death is actually a Christian heresy. The "true" Church doctrine holds that our souls do not separate from our bodies, but both body and soul remain together in the ground until the day of judgment—at which time all good Christians will rise from their graves in reconstituted bodies (with souls intact) and ascend into heaven, where they will live in God's presence for all eternity. But woe to all those dead who died without having confessed Jesus Christ as their Lord and Savior; these unfortunate pagans will also rise from their graves, but only to be sent directly to hell where they will be tortured for all eternity.

Another group of people with strong convictions about the afterlife are those who draw conclusions from the "near death" experiences of others. People such as Dr. Raymond Moody have documented many cases of people who claim to have experienced after-death states where they find themselves floating above their bodies while doctors are trying to revive them. More than a few of these people tell of being drawn toward a brilliant light at the end of a long dark tunnel where they may meet long dead relatives, or even find themselves in the presence of a divine being such as Jesus or the Buddha.

Modern science, on the other hand, denies that near-death experiences have anything to do with life after death. They point out that people who had these experiences did not, in fact, die, and almost dying is not the same thing as being dead. Explaining the near-death experience, researchers argue that the brain secretes certain chemicals as the body is shutting down, and these chemicals cause the dying person to have pleasant hallucinations. But when these hallucinations dim, researchers tell us, all brain activity ceases, and consciousness comes to an end.

Those scientists who do work on the human brain go further yet in telling us that none of their electronic instruments have ever measured any form of energy leaving the body at the time of death. As far as they are concerned, science has proven once and for all that there is no such thing as a human soul. In this, they agree with the Buddha: "When the body and mind dissolve, they do not exist anywhere, any more than musical notes lay heaped up anywhere."

Yet while Buddhists deny the existence of the human soul, they believe that there is some form of consciousness that experiences phenomena after death. And they also believe in "rebirth." But what is reborn? The Buddhist answer is that there are "samskaras," or collections of karmic tendencies and patterns that are attached to "us" during this lifetime. This core, or "mind-stream," because it still craves material existence, perceives phenomena after death in the same way it perceived phenomena while in a physical body. But because of the craving for material existence, these "mind- streams" are eventually drawn back into the material realm.

On the subject of death, there is one extremely important teaching that seems to be common to all four of the spiritual teachers in this book. Jesus, the Buddha, Krishna, and Lao Tzu make the point over and over again that the *fear* of death is the worst possible state of mind a person can be in at the moment of death. The fear of death, it would seem, affects what we perceive after we die. If we are fearless at the moment of death, we see death for what it is: just another illusion. In this case, we do not "taste" death. But for those with fear, the after-death state can be a nightmare.

Interestingly, this is precisely what those who have had near-death experiences tell us. For them, the fear of death no longer exists. Knowing this, they are able to live life more fully in the here and now.

Certainly the Buddhist and Hindu would agree. If there is no immortality in the usual sense of the term, neither is there "death." If nothing is born, nothing dies. Perhaps it is in this recognition that we come to realize that the fear of death is an inappropriate, and unnecessary, response to the dissolution of the human body.

When what gives life to a person leaves the body, the person is considered dead. But the spirit within the body remains.

Dialogue of the Savior

Of that which is born, death is inevitable. Of that which is dead, birth is inevitable. One should not grieve over what is inevitable.

The Bhagavad Gita

When the nature of something takes on form, it exists in relationship to all other forms. But when it ceases to exist in this form, it returns to its essential nature.

The Gospel of Mary [Magdalene]

All things in the beginning are un-manifested. In their intermediate state they are manifest. At the end, they are un-manifest once again. Why grieve over the essential nature of things?

The Bhagavad Gita

There is no point to running from death. Rather, death is your deliverance. No one who fears death can escape it.

The Apocryphon of James

We have existed in the past, we exist now, and we will exist in the future. The soul that has a body in this world will find another body after death. Those who know this are not deceived by the threat of death.

The Bhagavad Gita

There is nowhere you can hide from death—not in the skies, not in the mountains, not in the depths of the sea.

The Dhammapada

A Zen master was dying, and his disciples were grieving. "Why are you grieving?" the Zen master asked. "Because you will go away from us," the monks responded. To this, the Zen master replied, "But where would I go?"

The Buddha

One who has lived wisely does not fear death.

The Buddha

A body, while living, is soft and flexible. But when it dies it becomes rigid. Those things that are soft, then, belong to the living. Rigidity belongs to what is dead.

The Tao Te Ching

To be united with Tao is to be One. To be One is to live forever. Even though the body dissolves, the person who is One is safe.

The Tao Te Ching

Those who lived long ago did not fear death because they were not attached to life. They were happy when they were born and they did not resist death when it came. Their coming and going was easy.

Chuang Tzu

When one has completed his
designated time here,
his body will die,
but his soul will be alive.
He will transcend this world.

The Gospel of Judas

This world is the wheel of God to which all
beings cling. The world is the river of God,
and all of its streams eventually return to
Him. Around and around the individual
self goes, all the while believing itself to
be separate from everything else. Finally
the individual soul realizes its essential
unity with God, and achieves immortality.

The Shvetashvatara Upanishad

Judas asked, "Does the human spirit
die?" Jesus answered, "The spirit is
given to people on loan. But for those
who are enlightened, the spirit and the
soul will find their rest [in the All]."

The Gospel of Judas

Those who are in the body, but have
transcended [one's lower nature] is freed
from birth and death. He is freed from
suffering and achieves immortality.

The Bhagavad Gita

Jesus said, "I am returning to the place from
which I came. If you wish to follow me, you
may. But you will not enter the Kingdom
until you have perfected yourselves."

The Apocryphon of John

When the Self leaves the body it will
go to whatever the attention is focused
on at the time of death. Therefore,
remember Me at all times. With your mind
absorbed in Me, you will come to Me.

The Bhagavad Gita

DEATH AND IMMORTALITY

Death will claim those who pursue pleasure. But those who understand the dharma transcend death.

The Dhammapada

All things come together in Tao. Life and death are equal.

Chuang Tzu

The master found his disciple crying one day and said, "For whom are you crying?" If your sorrow is because you don't know where I am going, then tears are not necessary. If I didn't know where I was going, I wouldn't leave you. In the dharma, there is no coming and going, no birth and no death.

The Manual of Zen Discipline

He who lives in the Tao cannot be harmed by weapons. If he were attacked by a buffalo, the horns would find only emptiness. Were he attacked by a tiger, there would be nothing for the claws to sink into. For such a person, there is no opening for death.

The Tao Te Ching

You can only go beyond death by practicing faithfully and with diligence. Otherwise, you cannot escape death.

The Dhammapada

Those who are not attached to life will not fear death. They are more fortunate than those who give life too much meaning.

The Tao Te Ching

Jesus' disciples asked him, "When will we take our rest in the All, and when will the new world arrive?" Jesus answered, "What you seek, you already have within you, but you haven't recognized it."

The Gospel of Thomas

That which is unreal never exists. That which is real has never ceased to exist. One who knows this has discovered the truth. All things work in this way. The reality that exists within all things is indestructible. No one can destroy the Absolute.

The Bhagavad Gita

Whoever seeks to save his life will lose it, and whoever loses his life will preserve it.

The Gospel According to Mark;
parallels: *Matthew, Luke, John*

Anyone who thinks that the slayer and the slain are not one and the same does not understand.

The Bhagavad Gita

His disciples asked him, "Tell us about our end." Jesus answered, "Why do you want to know about the end, when you have yet to discover the beginning? Anyone who has recognized the beginning already knows the end, and he will never die."

The Gospel of Thomas

Those who understand that the Self is changeless and indestructible will never die.

The Bhagavad Gita

Fortunate are those who understand that they existed before they came into being.

The Gospel of Thomas

Those who see the Lord in all things understand that death is not real.

The Bhagavad Gita

The wise person knows about the coming and the going of consciousness. He knows that it comes from nowhere and returns to nowhere. It is devoid of reality.

The Buddha

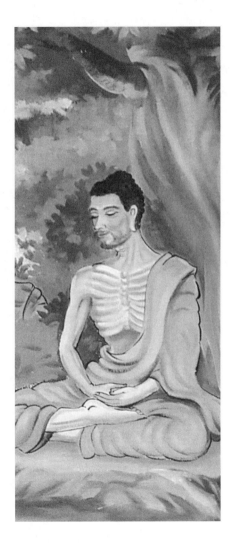

Death comes when least expected—often when a person's mind is distracted by something else. It is like a flood that comes in the night and carries away all those who are sleeping.

The Dhammapada

One who understands that life in the body is like a mirage is invulnerable to both temptation and death.

The Dhammapada

When the body and mind dissolve they are no longer in existence anywhere. That which comes into existence, comes from nowhere, then passes away again.

The Visuddhimagga Sutra

Anyone who understands the words
in this book will never die.

The Gospel of Thomas

Those who have taken refuge in
Me, and who focus on Me at the
time of death, will come to Me.

The Bhagavad Gita

Those who are awakened into the
Kingdom will never leave it.

The Apocryphon of James

The Self is changeless and un-manifested.
Those who know this need not mourn.

The Bhagavad Gita

When one wakes up from a dream,
he forgets all who he met there.
So it is with death and rebirth.

The Jara Sutra

The way to life is to be awakened. Fools
who sleep are already dead, but the
master who remains awake lives forever.

The Buddha

Enlightenment and Liberation

I have only one purpose: to make man free,
to urge him towards freedom; to help him
to break away from all limitations,
for that alone will give him eternal happiness,
will give him the unconditional realization of Self.

—J. Krishnamurti

The true mystic—the one who has finally, totally, and completely let go of the world—has but a single goal: to be united with the Source of his or her spiritual yearning. This Source of Being that draws each of us at our own speed has been called many things, and gone by many names. It has been spoken of, always imperfectly, by countless seekers—each trying to find the map that will show the Way home.

Jesus, Krishna, the Buddha, and Lao Tzu tell us that the Way, the map that points the direction back home, lies within ourselves. But they also correct our misperception that there is a destination. They insist that there is no map, no home, no pilgrimage, nothing to do, nowhere to go, nothing to achieve, and nobody to become. They tell us that we are already home; that we are already One; that we already live in the Kingdom of God. To see this for ourselves, we have only to drop the gossamer veil that separates us from our Beloved.

Like the human need for religion, the yearning to be reunited with the Ground of Being, the desire to take the Way that leads back "home," seems to be rooted in human consciousness, perhaps even encoded in our DNA. And yet yearning alone is not enough. Jesus, Buddha, Krishna, and Lao Tzu tell us that we will not achieve enlightenment, or attain liberation merely by hoping for it. While they can light the way, they can't take our journey for us.

As we near the end of this book, the reader may have realized, as I have, that it is not about many different things, but just one: freedom. And what is freedom but to be released from the shackles of our own making? The teachers whose words are recorded here offer us the greatest treasure in the world: freedom from the limitations of perception, freedom from the cares of the world, freedom from attachment, freedom from craving, freedom from doubt, freedom from karma, freedom from suffering, and freedom from fear.

In the end, though, all the words in this book are just words. They provide a window, not a door. The great spiritual beings of all ages tell us the same thing: "We can unlock your cage. We can open the door. But it is up to you to come out and fly away home."

I have defeated the world, so do not let the world defeat you. I am free of it. You, too, can be free of it.

The Gospel of the Savior

When lust and anger have been transcended, when your heart is under your control, when you have become self-realized, you are free—now and forevermore.

The Bhagavad Gita

Everyone who has heard and learned from the Father, comes to Me.

The Gospel According to John

He who acts for Me alone, who has Me as his goal, who is free from attachment, who is devoted to Me alone, and who holds nothing against anyone, he enters Me.

The Bhagavad Gita

When life's trials are at an end, and one is awakened, everything appears differently. This is attained by those who have overcome ignorance through knowledge. They have realized that life is no more than a dream.

The Gospel of Truth

Those who go beyond religion and seek Me, the Self, cross over the illusion to Me.

The Bhagavad Gita

Because you have renounced all things, endured all sufferings from one incarnation to the next, you have become pure light. Now you become king in the kingdom of Light.

The Pistis Sophia

Those who meditate on the ruler of all things—whose form can not be seen and whose essence cannot be known—passes through the fog of illusion into the sun of enlightenment.

The Bhagavad Gita

When freed from that which binds,
when the lust for life has come to
an end, one is not born again. He
is released now and forever.

The Sanskrit Dhammapada

When there are no more desires,
and no more needs, and nothing
attracts you, then you are free.

Chuang Tzu

When he has freed himself and understood
hidden knowledge, he crosses over to the
other shore. There he will stand on dry land.

The Catukka Nipata Pali Sutra

To know the Tao is to be enlightened.
To be one with Tao is bliss. Then you
may die, but you will not perish.

The Tao Te Ching

If wakefulness is always maintained,
then dreams pass away naturally.
When the mind ceases to discriminate,
all things become as one.

The Buddha

The mind which has attained wisdom and
peace becomes a mirror of all creation.

Chuang Tzu

The hero who has freed himself of
all that has bound him has achieved
peace. This one is enlightened.

The Itivuttaka Sutra

Like glass, polish your inner vision
until it becomes spotless.

The Tao Te Ching

One who has true knowledge of God
reaches the Father
and lives in Him forever.

The Sophia of Jesus Christ

Those who are perfected and have entered
Me will never again be born into this
transient body so burdened by suffering.

The Bhagavad Gita

Jesus said to his brother James, "When
your eyes are fully open and when you
are no longer blinded by ignorance, you
will have transcended this prison of flesh
and reached Him-Who-Is. You will cease
being James, and be the One-Who-Is."

The [First] *Apocalypse of James*

Those who are free from attachment,
fear, and anger—and who have
complete trust in Me—become Me.

The Bhagavad Gita

That which has imprisoned me is
conquered, ignorance has been dispelled,
all desires have come to an end, all
the cycles of forgetfulness have ceased
to exist. Free at last, I now receive
peace in the silence of eternity.

The Gospel of Mary [Magdalene]

All things return to Me; attaining
Me, there is no re-birth.

The Bhagavad Gita

Freedom is attained when all desires cease to exist. One who is free is aware that he is free, and also knows that he will never again come into this world. He has lived a holy life and did those things that were necessary to do. Now he is free forever.

The Fire Sermon

When one has freed himself from craving and attachments, he rejoices in his freedom. This one becomes a pure shining light that becomes the light of the world.

The Dhammapada

I have traveled through many incarnations looking for the builder of this house. Now he has been found, so this house will not be built again. Its walls have crumbled, its beams have fallen. No desire for it remains. I have reached the final destination.

The Dhammapada

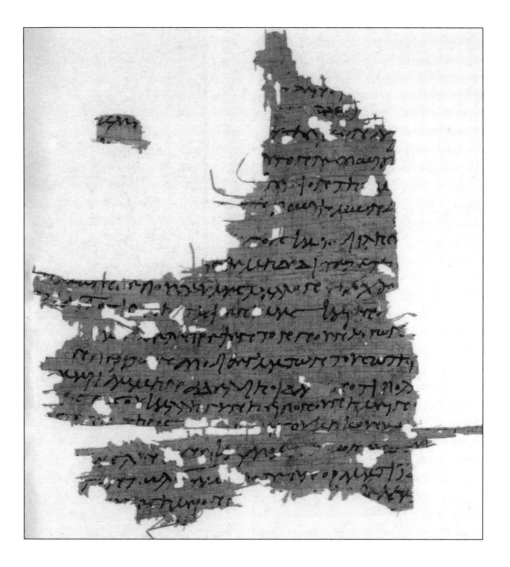

Final Words and Sources

The Parallel Sayings is a book that I have wanted to write ever since I recognized the connection between Gnostic Christianity and Eastern philosophy—three decades ago. But taking on such a project seemed daunting to me. Simply teasing out the parallel sayings from literally hundreds of ancient texts would, I knew, require a great deal of time. Dealing with multiple translations of texts would be yet another challenge. Still, I began collecting and categorizing sayings years ago, with the hope that I could one day assemble them into a book like this.

Another challenge I faced, and perhaps the reason no one else has yet attempted a project like this before, is the reality that most all English translations of texts written in other languages are under the copyright of translators and publishers. While it is possible to receive permission from a publisher to use a small number of quotations in a scholarly work, most publishers will not grant permission to use their translations for a book like *The Parallel Sayings* because they view such works as competition. The only recourse is for the author to do all the translating him or herself.

While I can still stumble my way through ancient Greek—the language the *New Testament* was written in, I do not know Coptic (the Gnostic Gospels) or Sanskrit (Hindu texts) or Pali (just one of the many languages in which Buddhist texts were written), so doing my own translations was out of the question.

Even if copyright issues were not a problem, there would still be the question of what translation of a text to use. Translations vary widely, and can be quite dissimilar from one another. The fact is that many translators take great liberties with a text, and do not even attempt to translate word for word—which can be frustrating to a scholar.

I think translators will also admit that something is always lost in translation, no matter if it is translated word for word, or not. Languages never translate exactly from one to another. In *New Testament* scholarship it is very important to be able to read the original text in Greek. Let me give you a couple of examples why understanding the original language makes a difference.

At the end of *The Gospel According to John* (21:15-17), the resurrected Jesus asks his disciple, Peter, if he loves him. Peter says, "Of course I love you." Then Jesus asks the question a second time, and Peter gives the same response. Then Jesus asks the question a *third* time, and Peter gives the same response yet again.

This passage won't make much sense to someone who just reads the English translation. The reader is likely to think that Jesus is being obtuse by asking Peter the same question over and over again. But while the passage makes little sense in English, it makes perfect sense in the original Greek.

The ancient Greeks had thirty-three different words for the single English word, "love," which tells us that the Greek language was full of nuance. Almost everyone is familiar with one of these words: "eros," meaning sexual love. The Greek *New Testament* used two other words for love: "agape," which means unconditional spiritual love, and "phileo," which refers to the kind of love friends share.

Armed with this knowledge, we can now read the Greek text of *John* in a new light. Jesus asks Peter if he loves ("agape") him, but Peter answers using the word "phileo." Jesus is asking for Peter's unconditional spiritual love, but Peter answers by saying, "Yes, I have *affection* for you." Jesus gives Peter a second chance to make good by asking the question again. But once again Peter fails to live up to Jesus' expectations. The third time Jesus asks Peter if he loves him, Jesus uses the word, "phileo," instead of "agape," signifying that he finally accepts Peter's limited love.

A more important example is *Luke* 17:20, where Jesus says that the kingdom of God is not something one can find by physically looking for it. Rather, the kingdom of God is *entos*, "within you." The Greek word, "entos," can be translated as either "among you" or "within you," but most Christian translators render the word "among you." Yet the *New Testament* scholar C. H. Dodd demonstrated many years ago that "entos" used in this particular context can *only* be translated as "within you."

Orthodox Christian theology has always insisted that the "kingdom of God" is something that will come in the future, at the end of time. But Jesus in *Luke* is clearly saying just the opposite. The kingdom is not *coming*, nor can it be observed, because it is already here! It exists in the heart of every human being. The version of this saying in *The Gospel of Thomas* has Jesus go one step further by stating, "The kingdom is within you *and* all around you." *Thomas'* Jesus believes that those with spiritual eyes are able to recognize the kingdom as being everywhere.

Ultimately I decided that the only way I could bring this book to fruition was to consult as many translations of a text as I could find, and then use none of them. Instead, I chose to reword them, but only after taking great pains to make sure that my wording was faithful to the meaning of the saying. In the case of the Gnostic and Apocryphal Gospels, following this process has also allowed me to illuminate otherwise cryptic sayings of Jesus that would be confusing to the reader in their original form.

CHRISTIAN/GNOSTIC CHRISTIAN SOURCES

The Gospel of Thomas

The Gospel of Thomas is attributed to the disciple Thomas—or more accurately, Judas Thomas, who in this work is identified as the "twin" brother of Jesus: "These are the secret words that the living Jesus spoke and Didymus Judas Thomas wrote down." Didymus in Greek means "twin," as does Thomas in Aramaic. But Judas Thomas must be understood as the spiritual, not physical, twin of Jesus.

Of all the ancient Christian texts that have been (re)discovered over the past two centuries, *The Gospel of Thomas* is by far the most important. What makes *Thomas* stand out above all other works is the fact that it contains a number of formerly "lost" sayings of the *historical* Jesus, which are not found in any of the canonical Gospels. Secondly, *Thomas* contains sayings of Jesus that have parallels in the canonical Gospels, but the Thomasian versions of these sayings have been shown to be the more original versions.

Three fragments from *The Gospel of Thomas*—written in Greek—were discovered at Oxyrhynchus, Egypt, during the nineteenth century. But the entire text of *Thomas*—written in Coptic—was discovered at Nag Hammadi, Egypt, in 1945, and is part of the famous Nag Hammadi Library. The Oxyrhynchus papyruses have been dated to the third century C.E., while the Nag Hammadi papyrus dates to the middle of the fourth century. The original text of *Thomas*, however, was written during the first century C.E.

Thomas' 114 logia, or *sayings* of Jesus, were compiled in two stages. The first layer of *Thomas* was written around 50 C.E., making it one of the earliest known compilations of Jesus' teachings. A second, and clearly Gnostic, layer was added to *Thomas* sometime around the end of the first century. The *Gospel* is attributed to the disciple Thomas, but like all early gospels, it was composed anonymously.

The Book of Thomas the Contender

Also discovered at Nag Hammadi, *The Book of Thomas the Contender* (or "spiritual athlete") is a revelation dialogue between the Christ—in a "revealed," non-physical, form— and his "twin," Judas Thomas. This document, along with *The Gospel of Thomas* and *The Acts of Thomas*, can be attributed to a Thomasian tradition that was primarily Gnostic Christian. The work was probably composed sometime during the second half of the second century.

The Gospel of Mary [Magdalene]

The only Gospel attributed to a female disciple of Jesus, *The Gospel of Mary* was discovered in 1896—in the possession of an Egyptian antiquities dealer, and is part of a compilation of texts known as *Codex Berolinensis 8502*, or the *Berlin Codex*. This codex also contained three other works: *The Acts of Peter, The Apocryphon of John*, and *The Sophia* [Wisdom] *of Jesus Christ*.

The Gospel of Mary is thought to have been produced in final form around 125 C.E., and is particularly important because it provides evidence of a struggle between matriarchal and patriarchal apostolic traditions in the early Church. Mary Magdalene's right to speak in Jesus' name in this text is challenged by Simon Peter and his brother, Andrew, who together represent the patriarchal viewpoint of orthodox Christianity.

The Church, founded on the patriarchal traditions of Peter and Paul, found it necessary to suppress the tradition of Mary Magdalene, and deny her—and all women—the right to preach and teach in the Church. Ten pages of *The Gospel According to Mary,* roughly half of the original work, are still missing.

The Acts of John

Even though it was considered heretical by the orthodox Church, *The Acts of John* has been handed down from ancient times through copying and recopying. *Acts* has some connection to Johannine literature in general, and may not have been in written form prior to the third or fourth century. Many scholars, however, believe that the "Hymn of Jesus"—known also as the "Round Dance of the Cross", and by other names—was part of a very early Christian ritual.

The Apocryphon of John

A copy of *The Apocryphon* [Secret Book] *of John* was discovered at Nag Hammadi, but two other versions of John are also extant. This work, most likely written during the second half of the second century, is clearly a Gnostic Christian text, and has little relationship with other works attributed to the disciple John.

The Book of John the Evangelist

Unknown prior to the twelve century, this text was probably written prior to the fourth century since it is clearly a Gnostic Christian treatise that attributes creation to Satan, rather than to the Hebrew God, Yahweh. Its theology about the Christ is also docetic: Jesus was not human, but was of heavenly origin.

The *Kerygmata Petrou*

The *Kerygmata Petrou*, or "teachings of Peter," are actually part of a much larger work known as the *Pseudo-Clementines* (works "falsely" attributed to Clement of Rome, the early second century bishop of the Catholic Church.) The *Pseudo-Clementines* have not come down through history in their original form, but derive from a basic document thought to have been written during the middle of the third century. The text of the *Kerygmata*, like much of the *Pseudo-Clementines*, is largely Gnostic in origin, yet goes back to the core of Jewish-Christianity. Among other elements, it includes a very revealing polemic against the self proclaimed apostle Paul.

The Gospel of Philip

The Gospel of Philip was discovered at Nag Hammadi and is not a Gospel in any true sense of the term. It contains only a few sayings attributed to Jesus, and is otherwise a theological exposition of the Valentinian school of Gnostic Christianity. It was written as late as the second half of the third century.

The Apocalypse of Peter

The Apocalypse of Peter is another text that was discovered at Nag Hammadi, and was also written during the third century. It is a revelation dialogue between the "living" Jesus and Peter. The *Apocalypse* deals at some length with the persecution of Jesus, and the Gnostic Christian understanding of his suffering. The anonymous author accuses the Church of being the true persecutor of the living Jesus.

The Apocryphon of James

The Apocryphon [Secret Book] *of James,* was discovered at Nag Hammadi in 1945. It takes the form of oral instructions given to Jesus' brother James, and to Simon Peter, by the risen Christ during the 550 days that preceded his ascension. Probably written during the early part of the second century, *The Apocryphon of James* shows Gnostic elements, but includes other early Christian material as well.

The [First] and [Second] *Apocalypse of James*

As with the *Apocryphon of James*, this text is attributed to James the Just. James was a Nazarene priest, the physical brother of Jesus, and leader of the early Jesus movement. Here, however, it is James' spiritual kinship with Jesus that is stressed. Both the first and second *Apocalypses* attributed to James were discovered at Nag Hammadi; thus both texts have Gnostic tendencies, while at the same time showing the influence of Jewish Christianity. Both *Apocalypses* attributed to James complement one another in stressing different aspects of the James tradition.

The Gospel of the Hebrews, The Gospel of the Nazarenes, and The Gospel of the Ebionites

These three Gospels no longer exist, even in fragmentary form. They are known only through the testimony of early Church fathers who quoted from them. The names of the Gospels in those writings are often interchangeable, but scholars have determined that the quotes come from three different Gospels. Because the Church patriarchs who quoted from these lost texts were the enemies of the Christians who used them, we cannot be sure that their quotes are accurate.

Each of these lost Gospels—like the canonicals—were narrative in style, and were probably written sometime during the first century. Jewish Christianity, the earliest form of this faith, was eventually condemned as heresy by the orthodox Church.

The *Didache* [Teaching of the Twelve Apostles]

Mentioned in the writings of Clement of Alexandria, a single manuscript of the *Didache*, dated 1056, was discovered in 1873. The text itself was probably written during the second half of the first century, although at least one important scholar dates it to middle of the first century. The *Didache* is an instruction manual for converts of an early Jewish-Christian community.

Dialogue of the Savior

The single extant manuscript of *Dialogue* was discovered at Nag Hammadi in 1945. The dialogue is between the risen Christ and several of his disciples. *Dialogue* was probably composed during the first half of the second century, although parts of it may be earlier. Generally considered a "Gnostic" Gospel, *Dialogue* shares some similarities and comparisons with *The Gospel of Thomas*, the canonical Gospels of *John* and *Matthew*, and *The Apocryphon of James*.

The Gospel of Eve

The only Gospel under the name of an *Old Testament* figure, this lost Gospel of Gnostic character is mentioned only in the writings of Epiphanius, and the quote that appears in this work is the only known reference.

The Gospel of the Savior

This formerly lost Gospel was discovered in 1967 among the possessions of a Dutch antiquities dealer, and now resides in the Berlin Egyptian Museum. After many years of study by scholars, the text was published in 1997. The remains of this Gospel are extremely fragmentary, but enough of the text remains for scholars to be able to state that it is probably of Gnostic Christian origin. While no date of composition has yet been determined, the manuscript was probably written no later than the beginning of the fourth century C.E.

The *Epistula Apostolorum* [The Letter of the Apostles]

Discovered in Cairo in 1895, and composed during the middle of the second century, *The Letter of the Apostles* is addressed to churches of "the four regions of the world." Its content is primarily orthodox—even anti-Gnostic at times—but still contains some

Gnostic motifs. The *Epistula* can be credited to a form of Hellenized Egyptian-Jewish Christianity.

The [Living] *Gospel of Mani, The Manichean Psalms* [Coptic Psalm Book], and *The Book of Mysteries*

These three works come from the third-century school of Manichaeism founded by the prophet Mani, and Mani himself may have written both the Gospel attributed to him, as well as *The Book of Mysteries*. A Persian mystic, the "arch-heretic" Mani fused Buddhism, Zoroastrianism, and elements of Christianity to establish a new religion that was so popular, and so widespread, that it rivaled Catholic Christianity. Manichaeism may be considered a major world religion, having existed in the East for centuries after it was suppressed in the West by the Church of Rome.

The *Sophia* [Wisdom] *of Jesus Christ*

Manuscripts of the *Sophia* were discovered both as part of the *Berlin Codex*, and again as part of the Nag Hammadi Library.

   A Gnostic revelation dialogue between the risen Christ and several of his disciples, the *Sophia* is a Christian reworking of a pagan text known as *Eugnostos the Blessed*, and may have been written as early as the second half of the first century.

The *Pistis Sophia* [Faith Wisdom]

A very lengthy revelation dialogue, the *Pistis Sophia (Codex Askewianus)* was discovered in a London bookstore in 1773. It consists of four sections or books. One section of the work is dated to the first half of the third century, while the other sections were composed later.

The Two Books of Jeu

As part of *Codex Brucianus (Bruce Codex)*, *The Two Books of Jeu* [Jesus] was rediscovered in 1769, in Thebes, Egypt. It has much in common with *Codex Askewianus* and is mentioned twice in the *Pistis Sophia*. Composed during the first half of the third century, this work is another Gnostic Christian revelation dialogue between the "living" Jesus and his disciples.

The Book of the Great Logos According to the Mystery

This title is the general heading for the manuscripts within the *Bruce Codex*—which contain *The Two Books of Jeu*.

The Gospel of Truth

A product of Valentinian Gnosticism, *The Gospel of Truth* was discovered at Nag Hammadi in 1945, and was referenced by the orthodox heresiologist Irenaeus, in his *Adversus Haereses*. Composed during the middle of the second century, this work may have been written by Valentinus himself.

The Naassene Psalm of the Soul

The Naassenes were an early Gnostic Christian "heretical" sect that the Church attacked through the writings of Irenaeus and Hippolytus. These heresiologists quoted from Naassene texts that are no longer extant. Our single quote comes from the writings of Hippolytus.

Mandaean Liturgy—from the Ginza

The Mandaeans, also known as Sabians, were generally thought to have founded their Gnostic sect prior to the formation of Christianity. Adherents claimed to be disciples of John the Baptist, and the sect itself has survived to the present day in Iran.

The Second Treatise of the Great Seth

Another revelation dialogue, this Gnostic Christian work was discovered at Nag Hammadi. Purporting to give the true history of Jesus, and concentrating on his torture and crucifixion, this text maintains the docetic nature of Jesus' appearance on Earth.

The Tripartite Tractate

From *Codex I* of the Nag Hammadi Library, this tractate is a text from the Valentinian school of Gnosticism, and was probably written sometime during the early part of the third century C.E. Rather than promoting the usual Valentinian Godhead composed of a masculine/feminine dyad, this text argues for a monadic first principle.

The Thunder: Perfect Mind

This unique document from the Nag Hammadi Library (but one that cannot be called Gnostic), was most likely used as a hymn. Its first-person style is feminine in nature. "Thunder" (feminine) *is* Perfect Mind, which suggests that the divine extends into the world. *Thunder*'s self-proclamation is in the "I am" style, and the verses are often antithetical or paradoxical. As such, it bears a close similarity to the "Hymn of Christ" from *The Acts of John*, parts of the Mandaean *Ginza*, *The Gospel of Eve*, and portions of the Hindu *Atharva-Veda*, *Svetasvatara Upanishad*, and *Bhagavad Gita*.

The Trimorphic Protennoia

Also found at Nag Hammadi, this text is also written in the feminine person, and also uses "I am" statements. *The Trimorphic Protennoia* ("first thought") consists of the Light that descends into darkness, the speech of Thought, and the Word or Logos of the Thought, which descends to earth and assumes human appearance. In its descriptions of the descent of the Logos, the text bears a striking resemblance to Johannine literature: namely *The Gospel According to John* and *The Apocryphon of John*. The first part of this text was not originally Christian, but underwent several stages of development. The last, and most Christian, revision was written no later than the middle of the second century.

The Gospel of the Egyptians

The apocryphal *Gospel of the Egyptians* is an altogether different work from *The Gospel of the Egyptians,* which is part of the Nag Hammadi Library. Almost nothing of it remains other than quotations found in Clement of Alexandria's work, *Stromateis III*. A number of early Church fathers mentioned this Gospel in their writings. Origen knew of it, Hippolytus wrote that it was used by the heretical Naassenes, and Epiphanius mentions that the Sabellians used it as well. *The Gospel of the Egyptians* was probably written during the first half of the second century.

GENERAL SOURCE TEXTS AND COLLECTIONS

New Testament Apocrypha, Volumes I & II, Wilhelm Schneemelcher, Editor, Revised Edition, Louisville, Westminster/John Knox Press, 1997.

The Apocryphal New Testament, M. R. James, Editor, London, Oxford University Press, 1976.

The Nag Hammadi Library, James M. Robinson, Editor, Revised edition, San Francisco, HarperSanFrancisco, 1990.

Pistis Sophia: A Gnostic Gospel, G.R.S. Mead, Editor, USA, Garber Communications, 1984.

The Didache: Ancient Christian Writers, New York, Paulist Press, 1948.

Gospel of the Savior, Charles W. Hedrick, Paul A. Mirecki, Sonoma, Polebridge Press, 1999.

The Complete Gospels, Robert J. Miller, Editor, Sonoma, Polebridge Press, 1994.

FOR FURTHER STUDY

Doresse, Jean, *The Secret Books of the Egyptian Gnostics*, New York, MJF Books, 1986.

Jonas, Hans, *The Gnostic Religion*, Boston, Beacon Hill, 1958.

King, Karen, *What Is Gnosticism?* Cambridge, Harvard University Press, 2003.

Koester, Helmut, *Ancient Christian Gospels*, Harrisburg, Trinity Press International, 1990.

Mead, G.R.S., *Fragments of a Faith Forgotten*, London, Theological Publishing Society, 1906.

Pagels, Elaine, *The Gnostic Gospels*, New York, Random House, 1979.

Appendix: Did Jesus Travel to Tibet?

*Those of us committed to promoting a better grasp of the
historical Jesus question today usually find ourselves busy
with the misconceptions of traditionally religious people,
but we must not avoid the very different,
and equally dubious, accounts of Jesus
popular in less traditional quarters.*

—Robert Price, Professor of Scriptural Studies at Johnnie Colemon Theological Seminary

I´m often asked about the story of Saint Issa, the nineteenth-century legend about Jesus traveling to Tibet to study with the Buddhist lamas there. Even though this legend was proven a hoax during its own day, New Agers have resuscitated it and insist that it is real history. The legend itself is fraudulent, but I can understand why people would want to believe it (or a similar one that has Jesus living in India). There are aspects of Jesus' teachings that make many people feel that he must have received an education in Eastern philosophy. And if it could be shown that Jesus' teachings were essentially the same as those of Krishna in Hinduism, and the Buddha in Buddhism, then one could make a legitimate argument that the Church has misrepresented Jesus for two thousand years.

But similar teachings do not necessarily suggest direct influence. Certainly the current New Age belief that Jesus traveled to Tibet to study with Tibetan lamas has no basis in fact. Historically, it is impossible: Buddhism didn't even arrive in Tibet until the seventh century.

Much of the speculation that Jesus traveled outside of his homeland has been based on a misconception about Gospel "history." People read Luke's story about Jesus appearing in the Temple at Jerusalem when he was twelve years old, and then wonder what he did from that age until the time he began to teach around the age of thirty. What happened to these "lost years" of Jesus?

Many readers are not aware that *New Testament* scholars long ago discounted Luke's story as a Christian myth, not history—as are Matthew and Luke's nativity stories. So Jesus' "lost years" include his entire life up until the moment he appeared on the scene to begin his ministry. Scholars concluded more than a century ago that the historical Jesus is buried under so many layers of Christian myth that we can know next to nothing about him as a historical person.

Virtually all reputable *New Testament* scholars recognize that the nativity stories and genealogies of Jesus are the myths of later Christians (like those who wrote *Matthew* and *Luke* around the end of the first century, C.E.) who wanted to tie Jesus to Israel's Messianic tradition that began with King David. New Age authors who claim that Jesus was married and had children who carried on his "royal blood line" are unaware that their new myths about Jesus are founded on very old myths.

The bottom line is simply this: Real historians know nothing at all about Jesus' life prior to the beginning of his ministry, and very little about him afterward. He appeared on the stage of history for no more than a year, and then he was crucified. If we speculate that he may have traveled to India or Tibet, then we might as well speculate that he traveled to Siberia or to the Americas to study with shamans.

In my opinion, no such conjectures are necessary to explain Jesus' teachings. If Jesus was an enlightened being like the Buddha, then his wisdom came from the very same Source. Jesus took the road less traveled: the road *within*.

THE HOAX OF SAINT ISSA

The nineteenth-century Saint Issa ("Issa" means "Jesus" in Arabic) hoax features a cast of very interesting characters. Playing the lead role is one Nicolas Notovitch, Russian Jew, Greek Orthodox convert, war correspondent, spy, bon vivant, and the author of *The Unknown Life of Jesus Christ*.

The book, published in 1894, was supposedly based on a two-volume manuscript Notovitch discovered at the Tibetan lamasery of Hemis in 1887, titled *The Life of Saint Issa*. Touring Tibet on horseback, Notovitch claimed that he fell from his horse one day and broke his leg, whereupon he was carried to the local lamasery to recover. It was here where he was shown the amazing Issa material.

Playing the role of foil to Notovitch was the great Orientalist Max Muller, editor of the famous *Sacred Books of the East* series. Muller, having read Notovitch's book, wrote to him and stated that, if the manuscripts he discovered were real, they would have been included in the Tibetan canon: The *Kanjur* and *Tanjure*—which, of course, they were not.

Muller also informed Notovitch that an unnamed English woman had sent him a letter stating that she had traveled to Leh in Ladakh, had gone to the lamasery to check out Notovitch's story, and was told by the abbot there that no such document existed. According to the letter, the abbot further stated that there was not a word of truth to Notovitch's story, that no Russian had ever come there, and that there was certainly no record of any Issa, Jesus, or Christ in any Tibetan literature.

Reeling from Muller's attack, Notovitch changed his story. In the preface to the 1895 edition of his book, Notovitch then claimed that he had written his book based on information gleaned from numerous fragments of many different Tibetan scrolls. There was no longer any mention of a two-volume manuscript.

This same year, Professor J. Archibald Douglas of Agra traveled to the Tibetan lamasery to interview the abbot as well. The abbot—who had been abbot there for fifteen years, and a monk for forty-two years—was outraged by Notovitch's claim. He called Saint Issa a hoax, and told Professor Douglas that Notovitch had never been to the lamasery, and there was so such manuscript.

For all intents and purposes, Nicolas Notovitch's book, *The Unknown Life of Jesus Christ* (in Tibet) was discredited, and the whole legend passed out of the public's consciousness—at least for awhile. But for a Hindu swami or a Buddhist lama teaching in the West during the early part of the twentieth century, the thought that Jesus may have been part of their religious heritage was tantalizing. To have proof that Jesus studied in the East would further validate Eastern philosophy, while encouraging dissatisfied Christians to convert to Hinduism or Buddhism.

In 1922, Swami Abhedananda—a disciple of the great Vedanta sage and mystic Ramakrishna, traveled to Hemis with the intention of discovering the truth of Notovitch's claims for himself. Supposedly, a lama showed the swami a manuscript like the one Nicolas Notovitch claimed to have seen. The swami wrote a book titled *Journey into Kashmir and Tibet*, in which he claimed that this was the case.

It's right about here where the historical record gets fuzzy. According to one account, Abhedananda translated the document himself. In another account, someone translated it for him. But no swami and no lama has even been able to produce a text for anyone else to examine. The abbot of Hemis himself denied the existence of any manuscripts about Jesus. Abhedananda's disciple, Prajnananda, admitted years later that when he went to the monastery and asked to see the manuscripts, he was told that the scrolls had disappeared!

In 1925, one Nicholas Roerich, a theosophist mystic and painter, visited Ladakh and supposedly heard tales about Saint Issa. But when Roerich quoted the texts he later claimed to have seen at the monastery at Hemis, his quotes were either identical to Notovitch's words, or came straight out of the book *The Aquarian Gospel of Jesus the Christ*—a "channeled" work written by Levi Dowling in 1908.

Notovitch's book was reprinted in 1926, and this stirred things up anew. A year later, Edgar J. Goodspeed wrote a book titled *Strange New Gospels*, subsequently expanded into two books: *Modern Apocrypha* and *Famous "Biblical" Hoaxes*. Goodspeed described in his books just how Notovitch's hoax had been created, and that seemed to end matters for a second time.

But you can't keep a good hoax down. In 1939, Dr. Elisabeth Caspari, who claimed to belong to a Mazdaznan sect (an invented modern reincarnation of Zoroastrianism) made yet another pilgrimage to the Hemis monastery. She and her companions later claimed that the lamas themselves presented her with books that revealed that Jesus had been there. But, of course, no one in her party could read the documents, so they really had no idea at all what they had seen.

Lacking any real evidence—an actual manuscript (or even photographs of it) that could be documented and studied—the image of a Tibetan Jesus still became holy dogma of first, the Theosophical Society; and second, the offshoot Summit University—aka Summit Lighthouse, aka The Church Universal and Triumphant, aka The Mighty I Am Movement, aka the cult of Elizabeth Claire Prophet.

And so it is with Saint Issa, the imaginary Tibetan Jesus who managed to study with Buddhist lamas six hundred years before there *were* Buddhist lamas. But lack of evidence and proof for something doesn't stop people for believing what they want to believe. Even though there is not a shred of evidence that a Saint Issa ever existed, the myth has become fact for many. Among New Age groups that have wholly accepted Notovitch's hoax as historical truth are Paramahansa Yogananda's Self-Realization Fellowship, the Sathya Sai Baba movement, the Hare Krishnas, and The Church Universal and Triumphant.

Certainly I can understand why all of these groups would like Saint Issa to have been real, and why they might wish for a Tibetan Jesus. But is it really necessary to manufacture hoaxes in order to connect Jesus with Hinduism and Buddhism? Aren't his teachings (including those in the Gnostic Gospels) enough to show that Jesus' spiritual philosophy had much in common with Hinduism and Buddhism? Orthodox Christians, of course, would argue against such a premise, but after having studied Jesus' teachings all my life, I believe that there are more similarities than differences.

When I was in college in San Francisco many years ago, I took a course on the *Bhagavad Gita* from a professor—a Caucasian woman—who was also a follower of the Vedanta school of Indian philosophy. On one occasion our class went on a field trip to the local Vedanta temple. In complete silence, students filed in and took their seats, the incense encouraging an attitude of reverence.

As I looked around, I saw something that surprised me: a large panel containing a row of bronze images of what I took to be great Indian saints. But there among them was one image that looked just like most people's conception of Jesus! When I asked my professor about this after the service, she replied, "Oh yes, Vedanta considers Jesus to be one of the world's great spiritual masters." Indeed, Hinduism believes that Jesus was an avatar. Apparently Jesus didn't have to travel to India or Tibet to receive this honor. He only had to be who he was.

(A special thanks to Robert M. Price, Jesus Seminar Fellow, and Professor of Biblical Criticism for the Center of Inquiry Institute, for compiling the above information on the Saint Issa hoax—first printed in The Fourth R, *a quarterly journal of the Westar Institute, Polebridge Press, Santa Rosa, California, May–June, 2001.)*